A Retreat With
Teresa of Avila

Living by Holy Wit

Gloria Hutchinson

ST. ANTHONY MESSENGER PRESS

Cincinnati, Ohio

Other titles in the
A Retreat With... *Series:*

A Retreat With Mary of Magdala and Augustine:
  Rejoicing in Human Sexuality, by Sidney Callahan

A Retreat With Oscar Romero and Dorothy Day:
  Walking With the Poor, by Marie Dennis

A Retreat With Our Lady, Dominic and Ignatius:
  Praying With Our Bodies, by Betsey Beckman,
  Nina O'Connor and J. Michael Sparough, S.J.

A Retreat With Our Lady of Guadalupe and Juan Diego:
  Heeding the Call, by Virgilio Elizondo and Friends

A Retreat With Pope John XXIII: Opening the Windows
  to Wisdom, by Alfred McBride, O. Praem.

A Retreat With Thea Bowman and Bede Abram: Leaning
  On the Lord, by Joseph A. Brown, S.J.

A Retreat With Therese of Lisieux: Loving Our Way Into
  Holiness, by Elizabeth Ruth Obbard, O.D.C.

A Retreat With Thomas Merton: Becoming Who We Are,
  by Dr. Anthony T. Padovano

DEDICATION

For my granddaughter
JESSICA BLAIR,
that she may be gifted
with holy wit

Contents

Introducing A Retreat With...

Twenty years ago I made a weekend retreat at a Franciscan house on the coast of New Hampshire. The retreat director's opening talk was as lively as a long-range weather forecast. He told us how completely God loves each one of us—without benefit of lively anecdotes or fresh insights.

As the friar rambled on, my inner critic kept up a sotto voce commentary: "I've heard all this before." "Wish he'd say something new that I could chew on." "That poor man really doesn't have much to say." Ever hungry for manna yet untasted, I devalued any experience of hearing the same old thing.

After a good night's sleep, I awoke feeling as peaceful as a traveler who has at last arrived safely home. I walked across the room toward the closet. On the way I passed the sink with its small framed mirror on the wall above. Something caught my eye like an unexpected presence. I turned, saw the reflection in the mirror and said aloud, "No wonder he loves me!"

This involuntary affirmation stunned me. What or whom had I seen in the mirror? When I looked again, it was "just me," an ordinary person with a lower-than-average reservoir of self-esteem. But I knew that in the initial vision I had seen God-in-me breaking through like a sudden sunrise.

At that moment I knew what it meant to be made in the divine image. I understood right down to my size eleven feet what it meant to be loved exactly as I was.

Only later did I connect this revelation with one granted to the Trappist monk-writer Thomas Merton. As he reports in *Conjectures of a Guilty Bystander*, while standing all unsuspecting on a street corner one day, he was overwhelmed by the "joy of being...a member of a race in which God Himself became incarnate.... There is no way of telling people that they are all walking around shining like the sun."

As an absentminded homemaker may leave a wedding ring on the kitchen windowsill, so I have often mislaid this precious conviction. But I have never forgotten that particular retreat. It persuaded me that the Spirit rushes in where it will. Not even a boring director or a judgmental retreatant can withstand the "violent wind" that "fills the entire house" where we dwell in expectation (see Acts 2:2).

So why deny ourselves any opportunity to come aside awhile and rest on holy ground? Why not withdraw from the daily web that keeps us muddled and wound? Wordsworth's complaint is ours as well: "The world is too much with us." There is no flu shot to protect us from infection by the skepticism of the media, the greed of commerce, the alienating influence of technology. We need retreats as the deer needs the running stream.

An Invitation

This book and its companions in the *A Retreat With...* series from St. Anthony Messenger Press are designed to meet that need. They are an invitation to choose as director some of the most powerful, appealing and wise mentors our faith tradition has to offer.

Our directors come from many countries, historical eras and schools of spirituality. At times they are teamed to sing in close harmony (for example, Francis de Sales, Jane de Chantal and Aelred of Rievaulx on spiritual friendship). Others are paired to kindle an illuminating fire from the friction of their differing views (such as Augustine of Hippo and Mary Magdalene on human sexuality). All have been chosen because, in their humanness and their holiness, they can help us grow in self-knowledge, discernment of God's will and maturity in the Spirit.

Inviting us into relationship with these saints and holy ones are inspired authors from today's world, women and men whose creative gifts open our windows to the Spirit's flow. As a motto for the authors of our series, we have borrowed the advice of Dom Frederick Dunne to the young Thomas Merton. Upon joining the Trappist monks, Merton wanted to sacrifice his writing activities lest they interfere with his contemplative vocation. Dom Frederick wisely advised, "Keep on writing books that make people love the spiritual life."

That is our motto. Our purpose is to foster (or strengthen) friendships between readers and retreat directors—friendships that feed the soul with wisdom, past and present. Like the scribe "trained for the kingdom of heaven," each author brings forth from his or her storeroom "what is new and what is old" (Matthew 13:52).

The Format

The pattern for each *A Retreat With...* remains the same; readers of one will be in familiar territory when they move on to the next. Each book is organized as a seven-session retreat that readers may adapt to their own schedules or to the needs of a group.

Day One begins with an anecdotal introduction called "Getting to Know Our Directors." Readers are given a telling glimpse of the guides with whom they will be sharing the retreat experience. A second section, "Placing Our Directors in Context," will enable retreatants to see the guides in their own historical, geographical, cultural and spiritual settings.

Having made the human link between seeker and guide, the authors go on to "Introducing Our Retreat Theme." This section clarifies how the guide(s) are especially suited to explore the theme and how the retreatant's spirituality can be nourished by it.

After an original "Opening Prayer" to breathe life into the day's reflection, the author, speaking with and through the mentor(s), will begin to spin out the theme. While focusing on the guide(s)' own words and experience, the author may also draw on Scripture, tradition, literature, art, music, psychology or contemporary events to illuminate the path.

Each day's session is followed by reflection questions designed to challenge, affirm and guide the reader in integrating the theme into daily life. A "Closing Prayer" brings the session full circle and provides a spark of inspiration for the reader to harbor until the next session.

Days Two through Six begin with "Coming Together in the Spirit" and follow a format similar to Day One. Day Seven weaves the entire retreat together, encourages a continuation of the mentoring relationship and concludes with "Deepening Your Acquaintance," an envoi to live the theme by God's grace, the director(s)' guidance and the retreatant's discernment. A closing section of Resources serves as a larder from which readers may draw enriching books, videos, cassettes and films.

We hope readers will experience at least one of those memorable "No wonder God loves me!" moments. And we hope that they will have "talked back" to the mentors, as good friends are wont to do.

A case in point: There was once a famous preacher who always drew a capacity crowd to the cathedral. Whenever he spoke, an eccentric old woman sat in the front pew directly beneath the pulpit. She took every opportunity to mumble complaints and contradictions— just loud enough for the preacher to catch the drift that he was not as wonderful as he was reputed to be. Others seated down front glowered at the woman and tried to shush her. But she went right on needling the preacher to her heart's content.

When the old woman died, the congregation was astounded at the depth and sincerity of the preacher's grief. Asked why he was so bereft, he responded, "Now who will help me to grow?"

All of our mentors in *A Retreat With...* are worthy guides. Yet none would seek retreatants who simply said, "Where you lead, I will follow. You're the expert." In truth, our directors provide only half the retreat's content. Readers themselves will generate the other half.

As general editor for the retreat series, I pray that readers will, by their questions, comments, doubts and decision-making, fertilize the seeds our mentors have planted.

And may the Spirit of God rush in to give the growth.

Gloria Hutchinson
Series Editor
Conversion of Saint Paul, 1995

Getting to Know Our Director

Introducing Teresa of Avila

She sounds like every other overextended professional woman in mid-life, who, at the peak of her powers, has said yes to more requests than she can handle. What wouldn't she do for a few days of pure, unadulterated leisure? But, knowing herself as well as she does, Madre Teresa can be sure that a vacation is as probable as a love affair. So she forces herself to take up her pen and do what needs to be done.

> But how disconnectedly I am writing! I am just like a person who does not know what she is doing. It is your fault, sisters, for I am doing this at your command. Read it as best you can, for I am writing it as best I can, and, if it is too bad, burn it....I have so little opportunity for writing that a week passes without my putting down a word, and so I forget what I have said and what I am going to say next.[1]

Teresa then admits that she is hiding behind excuses. She cautions the sisters not to follow her bad example since suffering without making excuses for ourselves is meritorious.

> Though I often teach you this, and by God's goodness you practise it, His Majesty has never granted this favour to me. May He be pleased to bestow it on me before I die.[2]

Here is a highly regarded religious reformer,

administrator, spiritual director and mystic who openly shares her mid-life memory loss, her inability to do what she exhorts others to do and her shortcomings as an author. These twin virtues of humility and humor characterize her as surely as the three tiny ornamental moles unfailingly mentioned by her biographers.

The Great Teresa, she of the broad forehead and expressive eyebrows, is as wise and wonderful a saint as anyone would want to meet. If she were to walk into the room at the moment, her aroma would be as appealing as that of brewed coffee on Sunday morning. We would soon see that she is brilliant yet practical, prayerful but not pious. Wedded to the Church, she is not blind to the egotism of certain theologians or the dictatorial nature of some hierarchs. A lover of sprightly conversation, she spends long hours in contemplative silence. A mystic and Doctor of the Church, she knows her way around a monastery kitchen and is not above haggling over the price of a piece of property.

Born Teresa de Ahumada y Cepeda (1515), she first sought the way of perfection at age seven when she recruited her brother Roderigo to join her in venturing forth to convert the Moors. She fully expected to be slaughtered by the "heathen." But that was the "bargain price" for entrance into heaven. "I want to see God, and to see Him we must die," she said, practical as a fishwife acknowledging the odorous consequences of her trade.

One of ten children born to Alonso Sanchez y Cepeda and Dona Beatriz de Ahumada, Teresa was the grandchild of a Jewish cloth merchant who was Christianized by political necessity. (Once the Catholic Church became dominant in Spain, the Jewish populace either converted or was expelled.) The family was assimilated into the "high society" of Avila where Alonso carried on his father's lucrative trade. By the time Teresa came along, they lived in an impressive home on the Plazuela de Santo Domingo where the Convento de Santa Teresa now stands.

Religiosity and willfulness characterized Teresa as a child. In her adolescence, however, adulation of the saints was superseded by more immediate passions. Like a modern teen soaking up soap operas, Teresa fed her fantasies with chivalrous tales and lavished her affections on male cousins. Her mother's death, when Teresa was fifteen, made her even more dependent on friendships that harmed her spiritual health. Don Alonso enrolled her in a boarding school where Dona Maria Briceno, a prayerful young nun, rekindled Teresa's love for the things of God.

Her deliberations about whether or not she should become a religious weakened her health, causing her to return to the care of her extended family. When she finally made her decision at age twenty, her father refused to give his consent. What he had desired in theory became too painful in practice. Losing the companionship of his charming daughter with her gift for lively conversation proved too much for Don Alonso. Teresa had to deceive him, sneaking away to the Carmelite Monastery of the Incarnation. She later wrote that the separation almost killed her.

At the Incarnation, Teresa joined some two hundred nuns, their servants and assorted relatives. She was happy to be spared "the slavery of marriage." The community celebrated the Divine Office, or Liturgy of the Hours, with great solemnity and attention to the rubrics. However, the practice of contemplation itself was short-changed. Teresa learned little about mental prayer. Once again ill health forced a departure. She suffered much at the hands of a quack engaged by her father. His ministrations left her a paralytic for three years until she was healed through the intercession of Saint Joseph.

Teresa returned to the Incarnation. For the next twenty years, the interior battle between her desire for a life of prayer and her natural attraction to the social life represented by frequent visitors at the parlor grille kept her divided. Many readers will empathize with Teresa's admission that "whenever I entered the oratory I used to feel so depressed that I had to summon up all my courage to make myself pray at all."[3]

Perhaps the image of a cloistered nun who has to force herself to pray will come as a surprise to some. C. S. Lewis would have understood perfectly. The author of *The Screwtape Letters* and many other books on prayer and spirituality, Lewis once compared his own reluctance to pray to a rose bush's unaccountable reluctance to bloom. "Shouldn't it want to?" he inquired.

Teresa of Avila did not hit her stride until she reached middle age. It was then that her years of perseverance in prayer, like certificates of deposit quietly earning interest, began to bear fruit. Secure in her relationship with the Lord, Teresa initiated a return to the austere Rule of Carmel. She founded the reformed Carmel of St. Joseph at Avila in 1562, despite vigorous opposition from members of her own order. She went on to establish sixteen more foundations for women and two for men.

In obedience to her confessors and her sisters, Madre Teresa recorded her spiritual progress in her *Autobiography*, *The Book of Foundations*, *The Way of Perfection* and *The Interior Castle*. While the *Castle*'s appeal is primarily to those advanced in contemplative prayer, *The Way of Perfection* is a fine handbook for beginners in mental prayer. Teresa defined mental prayer as friendly and frequent "solitary converse, with him who we know loves us." With this definition, she erases the illusory line between contemplative and active, or apostolic, religious, and even between religious and laity in the Church. Teresa of Avila remains one of the most popular and influential saints Catholicism has ever produced. Many worthy books have been written about her mystical experiences, her teachings on prayer and her timeless guidance of those seeking intimate union with God. In this retreat, however, we will narrow our focus in order to enjoy and profit from one of Teresa's outstanding gifts: her ability to live by holy wit. She mastered the art of living lightly and well. She had a well-trained tongue that not only "sustained the weary" but prompted healthful laughter. Her pungent observations have not been robbed by time of their flavor. They still have a juicy "bite."

A brief taste test of quips, adages and ironic complaints proves the point:

"It is bad enough...to be stupid by nature without trying to be stupid by grace" *(response to a nun who wanted to stifle any entertaining comments that occurred to her during recreation time)*.[4]

"Although we women are not of much use as counsellors, we are occasionally right..." *(said to a misguided cleric when her advice was right on target)*.[5]

"Better a bookworm than a fool!" *(to a prioress who complained of a nun's love for books)*.[6]

"When I fast, I fast. And when I eat partridge, I *eat* partridge!" *(to a critic of her gusty enjoyment of a good meal)*.[7]

"God gives other people nice dispositions precisely so that they may put up with such as he" *(said of tiresome brother-in-law)*.[8]

"Oh, if only your control over yourself were as complete as your control over others...!" *(to an overbearing prioress)*.[9]

"Know that if it is in the kitchen, the Lord walks

among the pots and pans..." *(consoling contemplatives assigned to active work).*[10]

"Don't grasp at comforts: it is only hired soldiers who expect to be paid by the day" *(against seeking rewards in Christ's service).*[11]

This is the voice we will soon hear throughout our seven-day retreat.

After traveling throughout the Spanish countryside in her exhausting efforts to establish reformed Carmelite houses, Madre Teresa was on her way to Avila when illness forced her to stay at Alba de Tormes (where some of the nuns had intuited that she would die). Unable to leave her bed, she realized that a new journey—free of "fleas, hobgoblins and bad roads"—was about to begin. Her companions wanted to know if she preferred that her body be returned to Avila after her death. Still irrepressible, Teresa quipped, "Won't they give me the charity of a little earth here?"

She slowly bled to death on October 4, 1582, of what may have been cancer of the uterus. By 1622, she had been declared a saint. Her mystical experiences and inspired writing persuaded Pope Paul VI in 1970 to name Teresa of Avila the first woman Doctor of the Church.

Her guidance has been sought by believers for almost five centuries. The pull of her vibrant personality remains strong. To any reader who gives her an attentive ear, Teresa offers a word worth remembering, relishing, putting to good use. We are in good hands for exploring the theme, "Living by Holy Wit."

Placing Our Director in Context

To understand Teresa of Avila, we need a passing acquaintance with her historical context. Her life (1515-1582) encompassed a time of transition and momentous change. The Renaissance was in full swing throughout Europe, effecting an artistic and scientific revolution of unprecedented scope. The Reformation, set off in 1517 by Martin Luther's ninety-five theses nailed to the Wittenburg Castle church door, had given birth to Protestantism. The Council of Trent (1545-1563), eagerly supported by Charles V of Spain, responded to the Reformation by dealing with many issues that had given rise to the revolt. Among the Council's unifying accomplishments was the publication of the Roman Catechism (1566).

By 1550, the Spanish had ended the centuries-old Moorish occupation of their country. Having conquered Mexico and colonized Florida, they were beginning to sense that such worldly conquests did not produce the happiness they expected from their exploits among the Indians of the New World. They were ripe for a spiritual rebirth, to which Teresa of Avila and her compatriots Ignatius of Loyola and John of the Cross would memorably contribute. Many longed not to explore the Pacific but to chart a new interior course through mental prayer and mystical union with Christ.

During the first half of Teresa's life, the Catholic reform in Spain had made great progress through the leadership of Toledo's Cardinal Jimenez. He worked to rid the monasteries of corruption, improve the quality of clerics and expand Catholic education. Jimenez founded the University of Alcala, which became a respected seat of learning and a bastion against Protestant inroads. In 1534, the founding of the Society of Jesus by Ignatius of Loyola further strengthened the Church by its commitment to defend the pope, evangelize abroad and promote education in Catholic Europe.

The arrival of the printing press about half a century before Teresa's birth meant that books on prayer and spirituality were available during her maturity. Unfortunately, she, who had received only two years' formal schooling, could not read the Scriptures. The Bible was printed in Latin only. However, Teresa had access to Spanish volumes that relied heavily on biblical quotation. After 1559 when the supreme inquisitor, Fernando Vales, published the Index of forbidden books, Teresa had a revelation that more than compensated her loss. Jesus told her that he himself would be for her "a living book." During the last fifteen years of her life, La Madre took to writing her own books in an inspired response to the vacuum created by the suppression of earlier authors like Johannes Tauler and Denis the Carthusian.

The Inquisition had been established in Spain in 1479 as a means of achieving political unity through religious uniformity. Fear of and intolerance toward foreigners characterized Teresa's time after centuries of peaceful coexistence between Christians, Moslems and Jews. La Madre's contemporaries also harbored what we would consider an unreasonable fear of the devil, a supernatural enemy who prowled about seeking unwary souls to devour. As daughters of Eve, women were seen as handmaids of the Evil One in their ability to tempt men away from the path of righteousness.

As Teresa once complained to the Lord, "Since the world's judges are sons of Adam and all of them men, there is no virtue in women that they do not hold suspect."[12]

The climate of fear and suspicion is verified by the Inquisition's thoroughness in sniffing out any semblance of heretical teaching or enmity toward Church or state.

Ignatius of Loyola, John of the Cross and Teresa herself
were questioned by this overzealous papal tribunal. Since
the Inquisition had the power to torture, imprison or
execute the "guilty," it may surprise those who do not
know her well to learn that Teresa of Avila was not
intimidated. When cautioned by friends to be very careful
about what she taught and wrote, La Madre observed:

> This amused me and made me laugh....And I said
> they shouldn't be afraid about these possible
> accusations, that it would be pretty bad for my soul
> if there were something in it of the sort that I should
> have to fear the Inquisition; that I thought if I have
> something to fear I'd go myself to seek out the
> Inquisitors; and if I were accused, the Lord would
> free me, and I would be the one to gain.[13]

This is the voice of a woman who held life lightly, trusted
in Jesus and had the sense not to fear what the world
might do to her. It is the voice of a woman who now
invites us to come aside with her in a seven-day retreat
where she will teach us how to live by the gift of holy wit.

Notes

[1] *The Way of Perfection, St. Teresa of Avila*, trans. E. Allison Peers
(Garden City, N.Y.: Doubleday, 1964), p. 111.

[2] Ibid.

[3] *The Autobiography of St. Teresa of Avila*, trans. E. Allison Peers
(Garden City, N.Y.: Doubleday, 1960), p. 112.

[4] John W. Donohue, "St. Teresa of Avila: The Grace of Pleasing,"
America, October 23, 1982, p. 230.

[5] E. Allison Peers, *Saint Teresa of Jesus and Other Essays and Addresses*
(London: Faber and Faber, 1953), p. 68.

[6] Deirdre Green, *Gold in the Crucible: Teresa of Avila and the Western
Mystical Tradition* (Dorset, England: Element, 1989), p. 177.

[7] Tessa Bielecki, *Holy Daring* (Rockport, Mass.: Element, 1994), p. 94.

[8] Peers, *Saint Teresa of Jesus*, p. 58.

[9] Ibid., p. 77.

[10] *The Collected Works of St. Teresa of Avila*, trans. Kieran Kavanagh, O.C.D., and Otilio Rodriguez, O.C.D., Vol. 3, *The Book of Her Foundations* (Washington, D.C.: ICS Publications, 1985), pp. 119-120.

[11] Peers, *Saint Teresa of Jesus*, p. 80.

[12] *The Way of Perfection*, p. 49.

[13] *Autobiography*, p. 311.

Day One

'Getting Real'
Humility

Introducing Our Retreat Theme

Living by holy wit was Teresa of Avila's strong suit.
First, she had an inborn ability to perceive reality and
respond accordingly. Second, she was adept at
discernment and ingenious in dealing with whatever life
imposed on her. (When life handed her a lemon, Teresa
made lemonade—often serving it up with a wisecrack or
two.) Third, she had the ability to see and sharply express
the ironic humor at the heart of our human experience.
Teresa knew that "people are funny" and often act
contrary to their own best interests. She appreciated the
incongruity between the way things are and the way they
should be.

It is Teresa's sense of humor, her skill at taking life
lightly and helping others to do likewise, that makes her
so endearing to many of us. She would have relished the
linguistic links in English between humor, *humus*
(roughly, "soil"), human and humility. It would not
surprise this author to discover that Teresa was one of
those G. K. Chesterton had in mind when he observed,
"Those who are marked with the Sign of the Cross go
gaily through the dark."

Opening Prayer

Through Your providence, Lord,
provide the necessary means by which
my soul may serve You at Your pleasure
rather than its own....
May this "I" die,
and may another live in me greater than I
and better for me than I, so that I may serve Him.[1]

RETREAT SESSION ONE

Because Teresa loved to laugh at the foibles and
lovable quirks of human nature, she would undoubtedly
relish the following story about true humility. It was first
told by David Casstevens, of the *Dallas Morning News*.

In a civil suit at South Bend, Indiana, back in the
forties, Frank Szymanski was among the witnesses called
to testify. The judge inquired whether Frank was on the
Notre Dame football team that particular year. The
witness said that he was. Asked what position he played,
Szymanski replied, "Center, your Honor." The judge then
wanted to know just how good a center the witness was.

Szymanski squirmed a bit but responded: "Sir, I'm
the best center Notre Dame has ever had." Later the
Notre Dame coach, Frank Leahy, who had been in the
courtroom, took his player aside. Knowing that
Szymanski was normally a modest guy who didn't go
around blowing his own horn, Leahy asked him why he
had made such a confident statement.

Turning red, Szymanski responded, "I hated to do it,
Coach. But, after all, I *was* under oath."[2]

Our retreat director would appreciate Frank

Szymanski's recognition that humility does not require us to think badly of ourselves or deny our God-given talents. Today Teresa reflects on what we might call the "get real" virtue. The humble have the power to see themselves clearly and to recognize their dependence on God, or as Jesus said to Teresa (in one of many locutions recorded in her books), "To know what you can do and what I can do."

To illustrate the dangers of false humility, which our Notre Dame center admirably avoided, Teresa tells us the story of a certain nun who resolved to become more humble. She decided that whenever a clever thought occurred to her during the Carmelites' recreation period, she would remain silent. Teresa immediately disabused the nun of that resolution. "For it is bad enough to be stupid by nature," she remarked, "without trying to be stupid by grace."

Just as we should not hide our admirable qualities under a bushel basket, Teresa cautions us about inflating our importance as the disciples of Jesus did when they argued about who was the greatest among them. She compares such squabbling about our relative importance to "the sound coming from an organ when the timing or measure is off." Teresa firmly advises: "God, by His Passion, delivered us from dwelling on such words or thoughts as, 'I have seniority,' 'I am older,' 'I have done more work,' 'the other is treated better than I.' If such thoughts come, they should be quickly cut off. If you dwell on them or begin to speak about them, the result is a pestilence from which great evils arise."[3]

When we are tempted to think that we have been unjustly blamed for something, humility urges us to think again. Forthright as always, Teresa says that "we can never be blamed unjustly, since we are always full of faults, and a just [person] falls seven times a day." If we are in touch with reality, we know that if we are not to blame for the specific offense named: "We are never wholly without blame in the way that our good Jesus was."[4]

Our mentor is speaking not of major offenses but of the daily misdemeanors that come with the territory of being human. A case in point: your husband or wife attributes the dent in the car door to your parking too close to others at the mall. However, he or she let you off scot-free when you carelessly backed into a telephone pole last month and roughed up the bumper. Although you were culpable only in the second instance, Teresa would prompt you to "take the heat" in the first as a practice in nondefensive humility.

Self-knowledge, our director insists, must be a primary concern of any Christian who hopes to grow in prayer, virtue and the mirroring of Christ in a world that • never sees enough of him. She calls it "the bread that must be eaten with every dish"; without it, we remain malnourished. Teresa notes how ignorant we would think someone who did not know his or her parents or country of origin. Then she adds:

> Well now, if this would be so extremely stupid, we are incomparably more so when we do not strive to know who we are, but limit ourselves to considering only roughly these bodies. Because we have heard and because our faith tells us so, we know we have souls. But we seldom consider the precious things that can be found in this soul, or who dwells in it, or its high value. Consequently, little effort is made to preserve its beauty. All our attention is taken up...with these bodies of ours.[5]

Although Teresa was beautiful in body and spirit, she did not take herself or her virtues too seriously. To do so would be to forget the origin of these assets. She recalls how many times she thought herself courageous enough to take on any mission God entrusted to her. And when the day of testing came, she proved worthy of it. However, on the very next day she would discover that she hadn't the courage "to kill an ant for God's sake if [she] were to meet any opposition about it." Experiences like these are the building blocks of self-knowledge. After re-reading some verses she had composed, Teresa once exclaimed, "What a brain for a foundress! But I can tell you I thought I had a great brain when I made up this."[6] Another time she lampooned herself, dryly observing, "It must be my nature—I could be suborned with a sardine."[7]

Because our mentor was often plagued by a variety of aches and pains, she knew well how these physical discomforts could consume too much of our attention—or even become a necessary part of our identity. If we have a sympathetic audience, we are all the more apt to concentrate on what Teresa terms "weaknesses and little illnesses." (We are not speaking here of chronic pain or serious sickness of any kind.) She administers a healthful dose of reality by remarking: "If you do not lose the habit of speaking and complaining about everything—unless you do so to God—you will never finish your lamenting....A fault this body has is that the more comfort we try to give it the more needs it discovers. It's amazing how much comfort it wants."[8]

Teresa would no doubt be wryly amused at the pharmacopoeia of over-the-counter remedies flashing across our TV screens every evening. Judging from that evidence, she would assume we are a nation of sicklings, constantly afflicted by headaches, backaches, hemorrhoidal aches, sore throats, sore feet, dry eyes, infected toenails, common colds and unbearable insomnia. Raising her prominent black eyebrows, she would surely say, "What did I tell you?"

Humility and self-knowledge should be prayed for daily with a trusting heart and a mind open to reality. Christ will not deny these gifts to anyone who asks, seeks and knocks in all sincerity. Teresa observes, "Knowing ourselves is something so important that I wouldn't want any relaxation ever in this regard, however high you may have climbed into the heavens. While we are on this earth nothing is more important to us than humility."[9]

A well-known story in which Teresa's humility—as well as her insight into human nature—is evident took place when she was appointed prioress at the Incarnation in Avila. Although the provincial superior wanted Teresa of Jesus to improve the community's spiritual health, many of the sisters had no desire to be reformed. They openly revolted against their new prioress.

Did Teresa storm off in a huff or impose her will on the community as less humble administrators may have? On the contrary, she came up with a memorable solution that contented everyone. She placed a statue of Our Lady in the prioress's stall in the choir. She then placed the keys of office in Mary's hands and sat down at her feet. Mission accomplished.

Throughout her autobiographical writings, Teresa tells us honestly of her faults, failures and lapses. Having struggled for so long to achieve spiritual maturity, she never forgot the years when she wavered repeatedly between God and the world.

> On the one side God called me, and on the other I followed the world. All divine things gave me great pleasure; yet those of the world held me prisoner. I seem to have wanted to reconcile two opposites as completely hostile, one to another, as the spiritual life and the joys, pleasures, and pastimes of the senses....When I was among the pleasures of the

world, I was saddened by the memory of what I owed to God, and my wordly affections disturbed me when I was with God.[10]

Teresa's frankness encourages us. For if so great a saint and so attractive a person was as "imperfect" as our mentor presents herself to be, how could there not be hope for all of us who—in our better moments—acknowledge sanctity as our ultimate goal?

In closing, here is a story told by Anthony de Mello, S.J., a twentieth-century retreat director with whom Teresa would have felt right at home:

A man goes to the doctor, complaining of a severe headache. Before the doctor can prescribe anything, he has to ask a few questions about the patient's habits. First, he inquires as to how much hard liquor the man drinks. Indignantly, the patient protests "I never touch the filthy stuff."

The doctor then inquires about smoking. Again, the man vehemently denies that he has ever so much as touched anything as disgusting as a cigarette. Undeterred, the doctor asks about nocturnal habits. Does the man perhaps do a lot of running around when his wife isn't looking? Even more insulted, the patient testifies that he is in bed with his wife every night by ten at the latest.

Armed with this information, the doctor asks if the pain in the patient's head is "a sharp, shooting kind of pain." The man replies that it is. "Simple, my dear fellow!" concludes the physician. "Your trouble is you have your halo on too tight. All we need to do for you is loosen it a bit."[11]

No wonder Teresa underscores the reality that without humility and self-knowledge "everything goes wrong." Their lack is the cause of "all our trials and disturbances"—and some of our headaches!

For Reflection

- *Are you a person who gets down on yourself when you fail to accomplish any great works for God? Listen to Teresa: "The Lord does not look so much at the magnitude of anything we do as at the love with which we do it."*[12]

- *Name at least three things you have done out of love for God in the past forty-eight hours. Acknowledge your goodness and give thanks to God for it.*

- *If you want to know yourself better but fear hearing the truth from spiritual friends or directors, begin praying daily for the power of humility. Listen to Teresa speaking to her friend Garcia de Toledo: "Disillusion me with truth."*

- *Recall one fault or sinful habit someone has pointed out to you. How might you begin to whittle down this obstacle to holiness? How will you show your appreciation to the person who disillusioned you with truth?*

- *Listen to the word of the Lord and make of it what you will.*

  And all of you must clothe yourselves with humility in your dealings with one another, for
  "God opposes the proud,
     but gives grace to the humble."[13]

Closing Prayer

Lord,
let me know myself
small and flawed,
yet great
in your reflected glory.

Gift me with holy wit
to know
what is real,
and laugh
at my littleness,
exult in your glory.
Amen.

Notes

[1] *Collected Works*, Vol. 1, *Soliloquies*, p. 462.

[2] Jack Canfield and Mark Victor Hansen, *Chicken Soup for the Soul* (Deerfield Beach, Fla.: Health Communications, Inc., 1993), p. 73.

[3] *The Way of Perfection*, p. 99.

[4] Ibid., p. 113.

[5] *Collected Works*, Vol. 2, *The Interior Castle*, 1.1.2.

[6] Peers, *Saint Teresa of Jesus*, p. 75.

[7] Ibid.

[8] *The Way of Perfection*, p. 48.

[9] Tessa Bielecki, *Teresa of Avila: Mystical Writings* (New York: Crossroad Publishing Co., 1994), p. 183.

[10] *The Life of Saint Teresa*, trans. J. M. Cohen (Harmondsworth: Penguin, 1957), pp. 57, 61.

[11] Anthony de Mello, S.J., *Taking Flight* (New York: Doubleday, 1988), pp. 114-115.

[12] Catharine Hughes, ed., *The Prison of Love: Selections from St. Teresa of Avila* (New York: Sheed & Ward, 1972), p. 21.

[13] 1 Peter 5:5 (NRSV).

DAY TWO

Getting Beyond Our Fears
Trust

Coming Together in the Spirit

Maryknoller Edward J. Quinn tells the story of a missioner priest (who insists on remaining anonymous) serving in Maswa, Tanzania. The priest watched with alarm as a termite mound near his rectory reached the impressive height of ten feet. He dreaded the day when the industrious termites would come to feast on his house. A defensive action seemed in order.

Determined to eradicate the pests, the missioner poured over five gallons of gasoline into their underground network. Then, standing off at a safe distance, he set a match to the long homemade fuse and waited in nervous anticipation. Thirty seconds later the explosion blasted the termite mound—and blew up half the rectory.[1]

Teresa of Avila, who entertained many fears of her own as she faced physical danger, hierarchical opposition, financial disaster, and the enmity of Carmelites who were threatened by her reform movement, would have commiserated with this threatened Maryknoller. She might have advised him, as she does us in her Soliloquies, "Let us try hard, let us trust hard."

And when the rectory gets blown sky high, let us laugh hard.

Defining Our Thematic Context

Teresa began by sharing her conviction that humility and self-knowledge are basic necessities of the spiritual life. They put us in touch with the reality of who we are and who our God is. Without self-knowledge, Christians fail to appreciate the beauty of their own souls; therefore, they do not make the necessary effort to preserve that beauty.

Today our mentor moves on to the virtue of trust. When a perceived threat appears, we are tempted to take matters into our own hands—without first consulting our Divine Protector. But the psalmist says, "For not in my bow do I trust,/nor can my sword save me."[2] When we misplace our trust, or indulge unnecessary fears, our ability to do God's work is derailed. Teresa speaks of how she learned to try hard and to trust hard.

Opening Prayer

O greatness of God! How You manifest Your power in giving courage to an ant! How true, my Lord, that it is not because of You that those who love You fail to do great works but because of our own cowardice...since we are never determined, but full of human prudence and a thousand fears. You, consequently, my God, do not do your marvelous and great works.... May it please Your Majesty that I render You some service and that I not have to render an accounting for all that I have received.[3]

Retreat Session Two

Teresa's hometown is a beautiful walled fortress through whose gates rode medieval knights and grandees ready to do battle with the enemies of Castile, the king or the pope. Atop Avila's eighty-eight towers perched keen-eyed archers ready to defend the city with their lives. Growing up in "the City of Knights," Teresa breathed in the spirit of chivalry, heroic deeds and conquests. She admired the knight's noble self-sacrifice, his courage and sense of honor. The true knight was, as Chaucer wrote, "of sovereign value in all eyes."

As an adult, Teresa was more than willing to become "a true knight of Jesus Christ" waging spiritual warfare against the devil and her own fears. Like her Spanish contemporary, Saint John of God, she recognized that victories of the spirit often required greater courage than those of the flesh. Once a group of Moors bullied John of God and taunted him for his foolish belief in miracles. They happened to be gathered around a fountain in the town square at the time. John, a burly ex-soldier, responded, "Is it not miracle enough that God constrains me not to throw you into the water?" That's the kind of conquest Teresa practiced and trained others to achieve.

The spiritual combatant's first step in getting beyond fear into trust is daily prayer, the mental prayer of "intimate sharing between friends." Whether we feel like it or not, seeking the companionship of Jesus in silent recollection and in "frequent solitary converse" with him is absolutely necessary. We should not shrink from the battle against distractions in prayer. Here it is not victory that matters but perseverance. Teresa advises that from the start we must be "very resolute" and "act like a person who lends something and expects to get it [recollection] back again." Resolve to give God a particular time of prayer every day, she says, and never "take it back again, whatever we may suffer through trials, annoyances or aridities." If we feel that we are failures at mental prayer, or that others have made much more progress than we have, we should remember that "humility is the principal virtue which must be practised by those who pray."

The path to trust leads through a forest of fears and anxieties. As a woman in an age and culture where women were neither educated nor prized for their skills outside the home, Teresa often felt inadequate to the spiritual campaigns Jesus required of her. She referred to herself as a "timorous creature" and exhorted her nuns to get beyond their feminine apprehensiveness. They were not to be like women at all but like strong men capable of doing whatever work God set before them. "If you do all that is in you, the Lord will make you so manly that men themselves will be amazed at you."[4]

Christians who expect little from God, or from themselves, are obstacles to their own growth. Teresa observes:

> Have great confidence, for it is necessary not to hold back one's desires, but to believe in God that if we try we shall little by little, even though it may not be soon, reach the state the saints did with His help...I marvel at how important it is to be courageous in striving for great things along this path.[5]

The knight of either sex who serves Christ must remember that "He is our model; whoever follows His counsels solely for the sake of pleasing Him has nothing to fear."[6] When Teresa was misguided by incompetent spiritual directors or scorned by those who thought her revelations were from the devil, she suffered much. But, for the most part, she kept a level head; at times, she defended herself with ironic humor. When the

Andalusian Calced Carmelites, who opposed the
primitive Reform, spread the rumor that Teresa was
departing for America, she quipped to a friend, "I
thought that was a beautiful idea about sending me to the
Indies.... God forgive them: the best thing they can do is
to say so many things at once that nothing they say will
be believed by anyone."[7] (As Teresa's compatriot, Saint
Ignatius of Loyola, said to his novices: "Laugh and grow
strong!")

In the following imagined dialogue between Teresa
and her beloved "comrade-in-arms," Fray Jeronimo
Gracian, we see how her holy wit sustained her through
the long campaign.

Gracian: La Madre, you were fifty-two when you set out
to make the Reform a reality. Many opposed you and one
sister denounced you to the Inquisition. How did you
respond to such obstacles?

Teresa: As I said to my brother Lorenzo, "These affairs of
ours do teach us what the world is like: really, it is as good
as a play!" On a more serious note, dear friend, I treasured
in my heart those words of Jesus to me: "Do not fear,
daughter; for I am, and I will not abandon you; do not
fear."[8]

Gracian: And did he indeed enable you to overcome the
womanish fears that threatened to halt your progress
repeatedly?

Teresa: Yes, indeed, although not always as quickly as I
would have liked. I remember praying, "O Jesus! How
many fears I have suffered before taking possession of
these foundations! I reflect on the fact that if one can feel
so much fear in doing something good, for the service of

God, what must be the fear of those who do evil, deeds that are against God and against neighbor? I don't know what they can gain or what satisfaction they can find as a counterbalance to all that fear."[9]

Gracian: So you never said "No" to him?

Teresa: "I read in a book that, if we forsake God when He wants us, we shall not find Him when we want Him."[10]

Gracian: Tell us the story of how you dealt with the fears of your companion, Sister Maria del Sacramento, when you were founding St. Joseph's in Salamanca. As I recall, you took over a house left in very bad condition by the university students who had boarded there. You and Sister Maria had to stay alone in that strange place on the night of your arrival?

Teresa: "The house was very large, was in a mess, and had many garrets. My companion couldn't get the students out of her mind, thinking that since they were so angry for having had to leave the house, one of them might be hidden there.... We locked ourselves in a room where there was some straw, which was the first thing I provided for the founding of the house, because in having straw we would have a bed."[11]

Gracian: And your companion spent the night peering fearfully all about her, expecting the worst.

Teresa: "Her thoughts then began to disturb me, for with my weak heart, not much was needed. I asked her why she was looking around since no one could get in there. She answered, 'Mother, I was wondering what would happen if I were to die now; what would you do here all alone?' If that had happened it would have been a hard thing for me to take. And I began to think a little about it and even became afraid. Because as for dead bodies, although I am not afraid of them, my heart gets weak even when I'm not alone. And since the tolling of the bells helped matters along [it was the vigil of All Souls]...the devil had a good means of making us squander our thoughts on trifles. When he sees that one has no fear of him, he looks for other devices. I said to her, 'Sister, when this happens, I'll think about what to do; now, let me sleep.'"[12]

Gracian: Bravo, La Madre! God gave you the wit to defuse foolish anxieties. How often we make ourselves suffer by indulging fears of catastrophes that never happen.

Teresa: I remember another night in an inn with no lamps, no food, and a leaky roof that allowed the rain to drench our beds. I tried to make the others more cheerful by saying, "Come now, take heart, these days are very meritorious for gaining heaven." And the mule driver, soaked to the skin, retorted, "I could have also gained heaven by staying home."[13] At least his sense of humor was dry.

Gracian: You did, of course, have cause for justified fear when the drivers became totally lost in the open countryside, when roads were flooded, and the time you narrowly escaped the running of the bulls at Medina del Campo. There was also the fear that your frequent illnesses would prevent you from completing your work. Yet you continued on in trust.

Teresa: "From what I now remember, fear of the hardship involved never prevented me from making a foundation even though I felt strong aversion to the traveling, especially the long journeys. But once we got started, the journey seemed easy to me, and I considered for whose service it was made and reflected that in that house the Lord would be praised and the Blessed Sacrament reserved."[14]

Gracian: Before we conclude, La Madre, I must mention how you lavished unnecessary fears on me, concerning yourself with my diet and whether I would kill myself in my frequent falls from those recalcitrant mules that I had not your skill at handling.

Teresa: I remember suggesting that they tie you to your mount to avoid certain disaster.

Gracian: That would have been somewhat uncomfortable, don't you agree?

Teresa: Yes, but as I once advised in a letter, "Don't grasp at comforts: it is only hired soldiers who expect to be paid by the day. Serve Him without pay, as grandees serve the King."[15]

Gracian: Ah, I am indeed well instructed. Adios, mi amiga, until we meet again.

Teresa's adventures (to be explored further on Day Six) illustrate the power of trust in accomplishing God's will. They also suggest that the knight who is armed with a sense of humor is an invincible opponent. As Mark Twain observed, "Against the assault of humor, nothing can stand."

For Reflection

- *Are you a person who generally feels fearful when faced with new situations, possibilities and challenges that may make physical, psychological and spiritual demands on you? Listen to Teresa:*

  "O greatness of God! How You manifest Your power in giving courage to an ant!"

- *Call to mind one time when you, through prayer and trust in God, overcame fear to accomplish some good. Relive this affirming experience in your imagination. Reflect on how you will try to be more open to God's power to transform an ant into a fearless lion.*

- *How have you observed (in real life, literature, videos) that a sense of humor can be an effective weapon in overcoming foolish or unnecessary fears? Listen to Teresa:*

  "On occasion I laugh at myself, and at other times I grow weary. An interior stirring incites me to some service—I'm not capable of any more...doing such lowly little things that it embarrasses me. [W]ere it not for the fact that the Lord accepted my desire, I saw that it had no importance—and I myself made fun of myself."[16]

- *Consider how you will integrate our mentor's example into your own reliance on humor as a defuser of fear.*

- *Listen to the word of the Lord and make of it what you will.*

  A glad heart makes a cheerful countenance,
  but by sorrow of heart the spirit is broken.[17]

Closing Prayer

Lord,
lead me
beyond my fears
into trust,
into strength-giving
laughter.
Let me try hard,
let me trust hard.
Amen.

Notes

¹ Edward J. Quinn, M.M., "Missioner Tales," *Maryknoll Magazine*, October 19, 1996, p. 4.

² Psalm 44:6.

³ *Collected Works*, Vol. 3, *Foundations*, p. 105.

⁴ *The Way of Perfection*, p. 79.

⁵ *Collected Works*, Vol. 1, *Life*, p. 123.

⁶ Ibid., p. 146.

⁷ Peers, *Saint Teresa of Jesus*, p. 76.

⁸ *Collected Works*, Vol. 1, *Life*, p. 221.

⁹ Ibid., Vol. 3, *Foundations*, p. 232.

¹⁰ Peers, *Saint Teresa of Jesus*, p. 80.

¹¹ *Collected Works*, Vol. 3, *Foundations*, p. 193.

¹² Ibid., p. 194.

¹³ Ibid., p. 52.

¹⁴ Ibid., p. 187.

¹⁵ Peers, *Saint Teresa of Jesus*, p. 80.

¹⁶ *Collected Works*, Vol. 1, *Life*, p.20.

¹⁷ Proverbs 15:13.

DAY THREE

Going for the Gusto
Joy

Coming Together in the Spirit

While we often leave home without our sense of
humor, the Holy Spirit never does. Witness this true story
told by Episcopal priest Robert Corin Morris.

A friend of Morris's, an inner-city clergyman, spotted
an unkempt Hispanic man lingering at the back of the
church after the midnight service on Christmas Eve.
Mark, the clergyman, cringed inwardly at the prospect of
having to deal with "one homeless person too many." His
experience and reputation as a compassionate pastor had
locked him into a situation from which he could not walk
away.

Nursing his anger at the injustice of it all, Mark
approached the homeless man and offered to take him to
the shelter. On the way, he realized he hadn't asked the
stranger his name. The man responded, "Hay-zoos"
(Jesus).

As Robert Morris concludes, "The ironic humor of the
whole situation suddenly washed over my friend. Here
he was griping to God about taking a man named Jesus to
a shelter on Christmas Eve! He felt as if it were a huge
cosmic trick! The comic aspect of it both judged his anger
and redeemed him out of it."[1]

The Lord's ironic humor was seldom lost on Teresa of

Avila, either. Here she was trying to found new convents dedicated to the primitive Rule, with its radical insistence on poverty, while being forced to haggle over real estate prices, maintenance costs, bequests and dowries. The more she longed to practice gospel poverty, the more embroiled she became in financial transactions. "So now that I have come to abhor money and business matters," she told her brother Lorenzo, "the Lord wills that I deal with nothing else, which is no small cross."[2]

Defining Our Thematic Context

Teresa has challenged us to become her comrades-in-arms by praying and practicing our way into the virtue of trust. On our spiritual shields we might inscribe her maxim: "Let us try hard, let us trust hard."

As readers have intuited, no retreat with Teresa of Avila can proceed too far before she picks up castenets, dances circles around us and invites us to share her joy. Our mentor knew how to "grab the gusto" of a Christ-focused life lived to the hilt. And she had little patience with believers who acted like their hairshirts were two sizes too small. "From sour-faced saints, good Lord deliver us!" was her emphatic prayer.

Opening Prayer

Be joyful, my soul,
for there is someone who
loves your God as He deserves.
Be joyful,
for there is someone who
knows His goodness and value.

Give thanks to Him,
for He has given us on earth
someone who thus knows Him,
as His only Son....
Don't let any earthly thing
be enough to separate you from
your delight, and rejoice in
the grandeur of God.[3]

Retreat Session Three

If Teresa of Avila had heard the following anecdote,
she would have passed it on to us: A man who is
exhausted all the time goes to a psychiatrist and is
diagnosed as a workaholic. Then he has to take a second
job to pay for the necessary treatment.

In her own words, Teresa puts it bluntly: "Anyone
who works all the year round badly needs relaxation."

When a Carmelite complained that the time the
sisters spent singing at recreation would be better spent
in contemplation, La Madre sent her to her room. "Don't
take this amiss," she remarked. "We need everything that
helps to make life bearable." Like Judas who resented
Mary of Bethany's lavish anointing of Jesus' feet with
"costly perfumed oil," the critical nun mistook an act of
love for a thoughtless waste of a valued "commodity,"
whether time or money. (See John 12:17.)

Despite her multiple responsibilities to various
religious communities, to her extended family and to a
wide network of friends and correspondents, Teresa took
the time to enjoy life. She knew that Jesus wanted no
"sour-faced saints" or cheerless workaholics in his

service. Her reflections on the Gospels assured her that the Lord did not deny himself the joys of communal meals, wedding feasts, holy leisure in the mountains or at sea, the companionship of men and women who loved him. Teresa saw no reason to do otherwise in the context of her vocation.

In the following dialogue with her brother Lorenzo de Cepeda, our retreat director reveals the ways in which she relished Jesus' gift of joy.

Lorenzo: Sister, do you remember how, when you were absent from Avila at Christmas in 1576, a group of your friends met to consider the meaning of the locution, "Seek yourself in me"? And how we each wrote our reflections and sent them to you for your critique?

Teresa: I took the opportunity to frame my response in the manner of satirical ceremonies held in our universities at the time. Doctoral candidates were treated to a round of jesting and raillery by their professors and students. Therefore, I warned you, "I have no intention of saying anything good about what the contestants have written."[4]

Lorenzo: As you said, you desired to enjoy yourself for awhile by composing "A Satirical Critique." You had particular fun with Fray John of the Cross, comparing him to an over-disciplined Jesuit. I think he wrote that we could not seek God until we were "dead to the world." And you replied...?

Teresa: That the "Magdalene was not dead to the world when she found him, nor was the Samaritan woman or the Canaanite woman." Then I added, "God deliver me from people so spiritual that they want to turn everything into perfect contemplation, no matter what. Nonetheless, we are grateful to him for having explained so well what we did not ask."[5]

Lorenzo: You did not, of course, spare your dear brother who had sent you such a pious reflection.

Teresa: No indeed. Of you I wrote, "If he has spoken of more than he understands, we pardon him—because of the recreation he has given us—for his little humility in getting into such sublime matters....Please God that since he is near the honey [St. Joseph's in Avila] something good will stick to him, for his answer gave me great consolation—although he was very right in being ashamed of it."[6]

Lorenzo: You gave us all cause for great jollity, Sister. In a similar manner, your response to a spiritual challenge from "the knights and the daughters of the Virgin"—most likely the Carmelite friars and nuns of Pastrana—won the day by breaking through the pious formalities with a flash of humor.

Teresa: I wrote "Teresa of Jesus says that to any knight of the Virgin who makes each day a very resolute act of willingness to suffer all his life from a superior who is wicked, vicious, gluttonous, and badly disposed to him she will give half of what she merits...in everything, which will be very little....This contract is valid for a month and a half."[7]

Lorenzo: Just as when you were a girl, people loved to be in your company because you were so lively and knew how to lighten others' burdens by making them laugh. I recall a letter you wrote to the Seville prioress contrasting the qualities of Teresita [Teresa's niece] and Bella [the little

sister of Gracian, Teresa's friend and spiritual director].
Like so many of your letters, it was for the
"entertainment" of the recipient.

Teresa: Yes, I praised Bella but said, "I have only one
trouble with her, and that is that I don't know what to do
about her mouth—it is a very hard mouth, and she has a
very harsh laugh, and is for ever laughing…. Don't say
anything about this to anyone, but it would amuse you if
you saw what a life I lead over controlling her mouth."[8]
(Teresa allowed a few young girls to live with the
community. Their youth and high spirits were considered
"no inconvenience—only profit.")

Lorenzo: You always loved children—not to mention little
adults.

Teresa: Ah, you refer, of course, to my beloved "half-
monk," John of the Cross and others whose slight stature
made them so appealing to me. When Fray John first
occupied the monastery at Medina, his impracticality
made me laugh. "It was only with clocks that he was well
provided, for he had five of them: this greatly amused me.
He told me they were meant as a help to follow the daily
schedule, which he wanted well fixed; I don't think he
even had any bed yet to sleep in."[9]

Lorenzo: You had the gift of appreciating others'
eccentricities rather than judging them. No doubt both
you and they were happier for it. In what other ways
would you say you savored life?

Teresa: Dear brother, as you know, I loved to dance and
sing on feast days and at recreation. I am delighted that
the drum and bells I played are kept in the museum at the

Convento de San Jose in Avila. Music was a source of great joy to me. I wrote devotional carols for your family at Christmas, remember?

Once when the nuns' habits became infested with lice, I prevented them from taking it too seriously by organizing a procession with musical instruments for which I had improvised one of my nonsense songs:

> "You've clothed us now in livery new, Heavenly King.
> Should creatures vile infest our frieze, Deliverance
>   bring!
> You who've come here prepared for death,
> Yield not one whit,
> And such vile creatures great or small,
> Fear not at all."[10]

The sisters carried a processional cross which we called "Christ of the Lice"—and that, too, is preserved at St. Joseph in Avila.

Lorenzo: You found joy where others might find only frustration. What other means did you employ in avoiding sadness and mining life's treasures?

Teresa: I loved writing prayers and poetry, making time for these pursuits even when I was overwhelmed with the responsibilities of my office. Here is a stanza from my poem, "In the Hands of God":

> Give me, if You will, prayer;
> Or let me know dryness,
> An abundance of devotion,
> Or if not, then barrenness.
> In you alone, Sovereign Majesty,
> I find my peace,
> *What do You want of me?*[11]

Lorenzo: I see how the arts gave you joy. You

recommended that we pray with icons. And didn't you once spend your last few ducats for religious paintings?

Teresa: When I founded St. Joseph's in Toledo, the negotiations with Alonso Alvarez were very tiresome. But when the governor gave me the license to go ahead, I was very happy. "It seemed to me I now had everything without having anything, for I must have had only about three or four ducats. With these I bought two paintings done on canvas (for I didn't have anything with an image to put on the altar), two straw mattresses and a woolen blanket."[12]

Lorenzo: You also found joy in contemplating nature?

Teresa: Oh, indeed. "It used to help me to look at a field, or water or flowers. These reminded me of the Creator—I mean, they awakened me, helped me to recollect myself and thus served me as a book."[13] To anyone who was having trouble praying, I advised "Go to some place where you can see the sky, and walk up and down a little."[14]

Lorenzo: So, dear Sister, am I to understand that although you once described your busy life as a "hurly-burly," you managed to reap a great deal of enjoyment out of it?

Teresa: His Majesty gave me the ability to appreciate life's incongruities. For instance, Lorenzo, I couldn't help laughing when you sent me money and sweetmeats and I sent you hairshirts in return! Despite my love for poverty, friends insisted on sending me quince jam, dog-fish and fancy embroidery. It really made me laugh. "I have a strange nature" and a flair for the ridiculous. God gave me the sense to celebrate life.

And when others criticized me for it, I simply said, "Don't take this amiss. [But] we need everything that helps to make life more bearable."[15]

We picture Teresa and Lorenzo walking off, arm-in-arm, laughing gaily as she tweaks his unexpected social advancement as "his Excellancy our senor brother Don Lorenzo."

Our mentor's admirable sense of humor and gift for celebration, whether she is feasting on fat partridge or composing a zany song about the lice crawling in her Carmelite habit, has given us much to consider. The workaholics among us may be in for an examination of conscience. And those who are easily defeated or made cynical by life's incongruities may consider a change of heart.

For Reflection

- *Are you a person who values prayer and work far above play and holy leisure? Seriousness and responsibility above a sense of humor and appreciation of how life is often "beyond our control"? Self-discipline and self-denial above the capacity to really enjoy good food, good art, creative activities and contemplating creation? Listen to Teresa:*

  "When I fast, I fast. And when I eat partridge, I *eat* partridge."

- *Decide on at least one way you will begin today to integrate Teresa of Avila's example into your own capacity to enjoy the life God has given you.*

- *Make a list of the ways in which you have "gone for the gusto" or experienced the joy of "life to the full." Next to each item, indicate whether you have experienced it seldom, occasionally, or often. Ask yourself: Do I have enough joy in my life? If not, why not? Do I secretly believe that I do not deserve it or haven't "earned it"? Listen to Teresa:*

"Be joyful, my soul,
for there is someone who
loves your God as He deserves."

- *Compose a prayer, a poem or a song expressing your desire to experience the fulfillment of Jesus' promise: "I came that they may have life, and have it abundantly" (John 10:10).*

- *Listen to the word of the Lord and make of it what you will.*

To make an apt answer is a joy to anyone,
    and a word in season, how good it is![16]

Closing Prayer

Lord, attune my heart
to life's contrarities,
quicken my mind
to elusive comedies,
tilt my spirit,
toward proffered joy.
Amen.

Notes

[1] The Rev. Robert Corin Morris, Director of Interweave Center for Spiritual Training, "God at Play in the World," *Weavings*, Vol. IX, No. 6, Nov./Dec. 1994, p. 9.

[2] *Collected Works*, Vol. 3, *Foundations*, p. 39.

[3] Ibid., Vol. 1, *Soliloquies*, p. 450.

4 Ibid., Vol. 3, *A Satirical Critique*, p. 360.

5 Ibid., pp. 360-361.

6 Ibid., p. 361.

7 Ibid., *Response to a Spiritual Challenge*, pp. 368-69.

8 Peers, *Saint Teresa of Jesus*, p. 61.

9 *Collected Works*, Vol. 3, *Foundations*, p. 16.

10 Bielecki, *Holy Daring*, p. 20.

11 *Collected Works*, Vol. 3, *Poetry*, p. 378.

12 Ibid., *Foundations*, p. 171.

13 Donohoe, p. 231.

14 Bielecki, *Holy Daring*, pp. 16-17.

15 Ibid, p. 22.

16 Proverbs 15:23.

DAY FOUR

Going for the Mark
Truth

Coming Together in the Spirit

Two monks in their travels came to the ford of a river.
There they saw a beautiful woman, elegantly dressed. She
could not cross the river without ruining her fine
ensemble. One monk immediately assessed the situation.
He then took the woman on his back, crossed the river
and set her down on the opposite shore. She thanked him
and went on her way.

The two monks walked on in silence for some time.
Then, the second monk, who could no longer restrain
himself, said: "Surely it is not right to touch a woman; it
is against the commandments to have close contact with
women; how can you go against the rules for monks?"
On he sputtered, venting his irritation. When silence
again descended, the first monk remarked, "I put her
down by the river. But you are still carrying her."[1]

Like the monk with holy wit, Teresa of Avila had
unerring accuracy in her aim at hidden faults that
prevented her friends from achieving full self-knowledge.
Out of love, she told them the truth they needed to know.

Defining Our Thematic Context

On Day Three, Teresa encouraged us to "go for the gusto" of a joyful Christian life. Although she herself was a hard worker, she would not allow duty to rob her of the time for play, creative pursuits, leisure, feasting and full-bodied celebration. No one could accuse her of being a "sour-faced saint."

Today we observe Teresa's gift for spiritual direction through forthright and often humorous truth telling. Just as she begged Garcia de Toledo to "disillusion me with truth," so she did for her loved ones. With Garcia and three others, she formed a spiritual self-improvement group "to free each other from illusion and to speak about how we might mend our ways and please God more since no one knows himself as well as others who observe him if they do so with love and concern for his progress."[2]

Opening Prayer

(On true spiritual friends)

Happy the souls that are loved
by such as these!
Happy the day on which they
came to know them!
O my Lord, wilt Thou not
grant me the favour of giving
me many who have such love
for me?
Truly, Lord, I would rather
have this than be loved by all
the kings and lords of the
world....[3]

Retreat Session Four

If the donkey carts in which Teresa traversed the Spanish countryside had sported bumper stickers, hers might have read: "The truth will set you free. But first it will run you through the wringer." Facing the truth about her own faults on the steep path to spiritual maturity had caused her a great deal of anguish. Who among us really wants to know that he or she is vain, impatient, self-concerned, dishonest, manipulative, overbearing, or otherwise less than perfect? With the help of several inspired spiritual directors (Saint Peter of Alcantara; Gaspar de Salazar, S.J.; Francisco de Salcedo; Garcia de Toledo and Jeronimo Gracian, among others), she did battle with interior foes.

It is amusing to note that several of her directors were not only younger than she but unable to grasp her mystical spirituality. For example, the Jesuit Baltasar Alvarez had only been ordained for a year when he was assigned to counsel Teresa. Years later he pointed to a large pile of books and confided to a confrere, "All those books I read in order to understand Teresa of Jesus."[4] For her part, Teresa understood the Jesuits well. She advised a young prioress, "But these Fathers expect to be obeyed.... Think out questions to ask them; the Fathers of the Company like to be asked questions."[5]

For those who seek self-knowledge, a good spiritual director must be found, Teresa insisted. The person must be prudent, experienced and learned; however, the first two qualities are more important than the third since a learned person can always be found to consult when necessary. A well-educated director is particularly helpful in clarifying the truths of Holy Scripture and advising directees to act accordingly. Teresa concludes: "From foolish devotions may God deliver us!"

Although Teresa had nothing but praise for good sermons as a source of spiritual direction, she was not deaf to the poor quality of some preaching. She points out:

> Even preachers nowadays phrase their sermons so as not to give offence. No doubt their intention is good too, and the work they do is good too, but they lead few people to amend their lives. How is it that there are not many who are led by sermons to forsake open sin? Do you know what I think? That it is because preachers have too much worldly wisdom. They are not like the Apostles, flinging it all aside and catching fire with love for God; and their flame gives little heat....[6]

Ever a loyal daughter of the Church, Teresa understood that it is an injustice to a loved one if we remain silent about perceived faults. When the situation required her to be circumspect or charmingly diplomatic (as with bishops or superiors), she employed masterful indirection to make her point. But she rarely missed an opportunity to set things straight. It is a tribute to her holy wit that even her antagonists were improved by her arrows of truth.

By listening in on the spiritual direction Teresa gave her contemporaries, we, too, may profit from her characteristic blend of maternal solicitude, pointed discernment, and what she would have called a "manly" ability to hit the bull's eye of another's wrongheadedness. Her deep perception of human nature may put us in mind of Saint Paul's complaint: "I do not understand my own actions. For I do not do what I want, but I do the very thing I hate."[7]

Teresa's insights are clustered under five thematic headings; each is followed by a few questions she might direct to us.

On Our Weakness

- "This human nature of ours is so *wretchedly* weak that, even while we are telling ourselves that there is nothing for us to make a fuss about, we imagine we are doing something virtuous, and begin to feel sorry for ourselves, particularly when we see that other people are sorry for us too."[8]

How might this insight apply to your family or community relationships? Does sympathy for your suffering of "injustices" weaken your commitment to virtue?

- "Hardly have we begun to imagine that our heads are aching than we stay away from choir, though that would not kill us either. One day we are absent because we had a headache some time ago; another day, because our head has just been aching again; and on the next three days in case it should ache once more."[9]

Although Teresa is speaking of avoiding daily communal prayer, might her insight also apply to the excuses we give ourselves for not persevering in justice and peace work or any other Christian commitment?

- "Let us try not to pamper ourselves, daughters [and sons]. We are quite well off here: there is only a single night for us to spend in this bad inn."[10]

Are there ways in which we make too much of minor sufferings, inconveniences, things that don't go our way? By complaining so readily, are we missing opportunities for spiritual growth?

On Our Prayer

- "What an amusing kind of progress in the love of God it is, to tie His hands by thinking that He cannot help us except by one path!"[11]

  Speaking to her Carmelite sisters, Teresa corrects their desire to persist in prayer that pleases them rather than "go after something that matters" to God. Do we sometimes insist on the prayer of rest when the prayer of action is called for? Or do we require one particular answer to our prayer of petition?

- "We cannot be at prayer all the time....With regard to your sleep, I will tell you—indeed I will order you—not to take less than six hours. Remember that we middle-aged people need to treat our bodies well so as not to wreck the spirit, which is a terrible trial.... How silly of you to think that the prayer you are experiencing is the kind that kept me awake! It has nothing to do with it: I was trying far harder to go to sleep than to keep awake."[12]

  Teresa advises her younger brother Lorenzo against trying to live like a monk when he is a family man with many responsibilities in the world. Are there ways in which we try to imitate those whose vocation we consider "higher" than ours? Are we unwittingly supporting a spiritual caste system that is unhealthful for us and the Church?

- "Believe me, Martha and Mary must join together in order to show hospitality to the Lord and have Him always present and not host Him badly by failing to give Him something to eat. How would Mary, always seated at His feet, provide Him with food if her sister did not help her?"[13]

Teresa again corrects a false dichotomy between contemplatives and active servants of the Lord. Are we integrating both into our daily spiritual practice?

- "Those of you who cannot engage in much discursive reflection with the intellect or keep your mind from distraction, get used to this practice! Get used to it! See, I know that you can do this; for I suffered many years from the trial...of not being able to quiet the mind in anything. But I know that the Lord does not leave us so abandoned; for if we humbly ask Him for this friendship, He will not deny it to us. And if we cannot succeed in one year, we will succeed later. Let's not regret the time that is so well spent. Who's making us hurry?"[14]

Our director will not countenance rationalizations about why we do not practice mental prayer or recollected "friendly intercourse" with God. Her bold correction has a contemporary ring to it: "Get used to it!" Will we?

On Being Too Spiritual

- "I was amused that [you are] now wanting more trials again.

  "Do, for the love of God, let us have a little respite—for they involve others beside yourself! Let us give them a few days' rest!"[15]

Teresa is correcting Jeronimo Gracian's seeking more trials than God has clearly sent him. Do we at times let ourselves in for unnecessary suffering out of false piety or a suspicion that we deserve to suffer more? How does this affect our loved ones?

- "Well, come now, my daughters, don't be sad when obedience draws you to involvement in exterior matters. Know that if it is in the kitchen, the Lord walks among the pots and pans."[16]

Do we often resent "menial" or routine work that takes us away from more meaningful or spiritual pursuits? What might Jesus tell us about this false dichotomy?

■ "For even when she [the prioress of St. Joseph's in Toledo] said something only casually, they [her devoted sisters] would immediately carry it out. Once they were looking at a pond that was in the garden, and she said to a nun standing nearby: 'But what would happen if I were to say, "jump in"?'

"Hardly was this said, and the nun was in the pond and got so soaked that she had to change her clothes."[17]

As we laugh at this hapless nun, are we missing any point about blind obedience to authority in the Church, family or society? Do we sometimes abdicate our responsibility to act out of the mature Christian freedom Jesus entrusted to us?

On Pride and Egotism

■ "Your Reverence must not be so clever.... It is a great mistake to think you know everything, and then say you are humble. As if it were not enough that you should be self-willed yourself, you have to teach the other nuns to be so too.... I cannot think where you get so much vanity from to give you all that rashness."[18]

Maria Bautista, prioress at Valladolid, was dearly loved by Teresa. Here La Madre takes direct aim at Maria's vanity and false humility. Are we as willing to express our love for our friends or family by enabling them to see where pride or egotism are leading them astray?

- "Oh, if only your control over yourself were as complete as your control over others, how lightly you would esteem what this world calls trials!"[19]

  Addressed to Dona Maria de Mendoza, an aristocrat whose education provided an even greater sense of superiority, Teresa's correction applies to all who, in any way, "lord it over" others and fail to progress in self-control.

- "Let your Reverence remember that children are apt to err, and that fathers must not look at their faults, but forgive them. For the love of Our Lord, I beseech your Reverence to do me this favour.... Although we women are not of much use as counsellors, we are occasionally right...."[20]

  Using gentle persuasion and velvet irony, Teresa corrects the Carmelite Superior General Rubeo for his unjust treatment of two friars. Are we forgiving of those who are under our authority? Do we heed those who counsel compassion?

- "I am dreadfully sorry for my sister—we have a great deal to put up with in him.... God gives other people nice dispositions precisely so that they may put up with such as he."[21]

  Teresa commiserates with Lorenzo about their self-centered brother-in-law Ovalle. Thus, she gives us an opportunity to ask: Am I, in any way, a trial to my family or community? How might I give them a break?

On Women

- "I was amused at your remark that you could sum her up immediately if you once saw her. We women cannot be summed up as easily as that."[22]

Speaking to Ambrosio Mariano who presumes he can judge who will make an acceptable Carmelite candidate, Teresa tweaks him for his prejudicial presumption. Do we need to examine our own attitudes about women—particularly in the Church?

- "They say that for a woman to be a good wife toward her husband she must be sad when he is sad, and joyful when he is joyful, even though she may not be so. (See, what subjection you have been freed from, Sisters!)"[23]

Although Teresa's example seems exaggerated, her point about a lack of equality between marriage partners is not outdated in today's world. How are we working to move beyond any subjection of women—or men—in marriage?

- "Nor did you, Lord, when you walked in the world, despise women: rather, You always, with great compassion, helped them. And You found as much love and more faith in them than You did in men.... Since the world's judges are sons of Adam and all of them are men, there is no virtue in women they do not hold suspect.... These are times in which it would be wrong to undervalue virtuous and strong souls, even though they are women."[24]

How are we working to move beyond any undervaluing of women in Church or society?

Teresa encourages us to consider which of these arrows of truth apply to us, and which, after prayer and thoughtful consideration, we may be called to aim at those whose spiritual welfare we desire. Do we love them enough to "disillusion them with truth?"

For Reflection

- *How have you (or will you) make finding a good spiritual director, gifted with holy wit, a priority in your life? Listen to Teresa:*

  "It should be possible to find a number of people who combine both learning and spirituality, and the more favours the Lord grants you in prayer, the more needful is it that your good works and your prayers should have a sure foundation."[25]

- *Have you ever helped someone to see the truth about himself or herself by employing constructive humor? Recall the incident(s). How might you sharpen this skill by prayer and practice?*

- *Listen to the word of the Lord and make of it what you will.*

  "If another member of the church sins against you, go and point out the fault when the two of you are alone. If the member listens to you, you have regained that one."[26]

Closing Prayer

Lord,
enable me
to bear the sting
of corrective arrows,
and aim with love.
Amen.

Notes

[1] Irmgard Schoegl, trans., *The Wisdom of the Zen Masters* (New York: New Directions, 1975), p. 39.

[2] *Collected Works*, Vol. 1, *Life*, 16.7.

[3] *The Way of Perfection*, p. 75.

[4] *Collected Works*, Vol. 1, *Life*, p. 34.

[5] Mary Purcell, "Teresa of Avila," in *Saints for All Seasons*, John J. Delaney, ed. (Garden City: Doubleday, 1978), p. 124.

[6] *Autobiography*, pp. 166-67.

[7] Romans 7:15.

[8] *The Way of Perfection*, pp. 102-03.

[9] Ibid., p. 92.

[10] Ibid. p. 266

[11] *Collected Works*, Vol. 3, *Foundations*, p. 118.

[12] Bielecki, *Holy Daring*, pp. 18-19.

[13] *Collected Works*, Vol. 2, *Interior Castle*, 7.4.12.

[14] Ibid., Way, 26.2.

[15] Bielecki, *Holy Daring*, p. 23.

[16] *Collected Works*, Vol. 3, *Foundations*, pp. 119-120.

[17] Ibid., pp. 176-77.

[18] Bielecki, *Mystical Writings*, p. 62.

[19] Peers, *Saint Teresa of Jesus*, p. 77.

[20] Ibid., p. 68.

[21] Ibid., p. 58.

[22] Bielecki, *Mystical Writings*, p. 70.

[23] *Collected Works, Way*, 26.4.

[24] Ibid., 3-7

[25] *The Way of Perfection*, p. 63

[26] Matthew 18:15.

Day Five

Giving Our Hearts
Love

Coming Together in the Spirit

It happened in the L'Arche Daybreak Community in Toronto where people with mental and physical disabilities live together with their assistants. An argument broke out when a member of the community challenged Paul to clean up before coming to the table. Because he had been working in the barn, his clothes smelled of straw and manure. However, he responded that "this was his house and he could decide for himself when he would shower." The antagonism between the two made the others nervous, ruining their peaceful meal.

When everyone had left the table, Frank (a community member) took the person who had challenged Paul aside and commented, "So, you and Paul are not doing very well!" The community member politely told Frank to mind his own business, saying, "Paul and I have to sort that out!" However, Frank was not deterred. He looked into his friend's eyes and quietly said, "You know, if you want to help Paul, you have to love him."[1]

Defining Our Thematic Context

Frank may never have read Teresa of Avila. But she

would have heartily approved of his approach to spiritual direction or correction of others in the Christian community. As we saw on Day Four, she aimed her arrows of truth with an accuracy born of "tough love."

In today's session, Teresa expresses herself more extensively on the virtue of love, a power that she used widely, sometimes foolishly, always generously. Her holy wit made her loveable. It also made her more resilient when others invariably failed her in fulfilling love's demands. "All must be friends, all must be loved, all be held dear," she observed.

Opening Prayer

> If the love You have for me,
> Is like the love I have for
> You,
> My God, what detains me?
> Oh, what is delaying You?
> ....
> One all possessing love I ask
> My God, my soul centered in You,
> Making a delightful nest,
> A resting place most pleasing.[2]

RETREAT SESSION FIVE

A story in the *Spirituality of Imperfection* illustrates the kind of devotion Teresa approved of—even though she might have disapproved of the socially unacceptable language in which it is expressed.

When Mohammed was reciting morning prayer in the

mosque one day, he proclaimed the verse in which Pharaoh asserts, "I am your true God." Among those present that morning was a zealous young Arab aspirant, who, upon hearing those words, shattered the silence with a spontaneous shout, "The boastful son of a bitch!"

Mohammed continued with the prayer, making no sign that he had heard the aspirant's outburst. Later the other worshipers corrected the aspirant, saying that he had surely offended God by his vile language in the Prophet's presence.

The chastened aspirant felt terrible about his unpremeditated offense. Then the angel Gabriel appeared to Mohammed to deliver a message from God. "God sends greetings to you and wishes you to get these people to stop scolding that simple Arab; indeed, his spontaneous profanity moved my heart more than the holy prayers of the others."[3]

Forthrightness in expressing her love for God and others is as characteristic of Teresa as her ready wit. She once said, "The Lord gave me the grace of pleasing." And she pleased people of every description by not hiding her affection for them—even though her honesty increased her vulnerability. Like Saint Augustine and Thomas Merton, Teresa attracts readers through the confessional nature of her autobiographical writing. She allows us to see how foolishly and extravagantly she sometimes loved those from whom she should have practiced a degree of detachment. But these revelations simply draw us closer to one who shares our humanity so openly. As Merton observed, "Before you can be a saint, you have got to be human."

In a dialogue with her dear friend, Maria de San Jose, prioress of Seville, Teresa reflects on love as she experienced this core virtue.

Maria: We begin with Jesus because I know you would have it no other way, La Madre. He was your constant companion and the source of your love for others.

Teresa: "What more do we desire than to have such a good friend at our side, who will not abandon us in our labors and tribulations, as friends in the world do? Blessed are they who truly love Him and always keep Him at their side!"[4]

Maria: I remember how often you assured beginners in mental prayer that the important thing was not to think much but to love much. You said we should do that which best stirred us to love.

Teresa: But "[p]erhaps we don't know what love is. I wouldn't be surprised because it doesn't consist in great delight but in desiring with strong determination to please God in everything, in striving, insofar as possible, not to offend Him, and in asking Him for the advancement of the honor and glory of His Son."[5]

Maria: And how can we, in our weakness, know that we are indeed doing so?

Teresa: "We cannot be sure if we are loving God, although we may have good reasons for believing that we are, but we can know quite well if we are loving our neighbor."[6]

Maria: And I for one can testify, La Madre, that you loved your neighbor well—even when some of us, by our temperaments or conflicting habits, drove you to distraction!

Teresa: Oh, Maria, how your moodiness and vanity and

secretiveness at times made it nearly impossible for me to work with you! Yet your generosity and unreserved affection always prompted me to forgive any offenses on the spot. As I told you, "Provided you love me as much as I love you, I forgive you everything, whether in the past or in the future."[7]

Maria: Those were your very words. And I must confess I thought them a bit rash at the time.

Teresa: Oh, how often was I accused of loving rashly—or worse! Even when I was an old woman, the gossips buzzed about my "love affairs" with my spiritual directors. They could not differentiate between carnal and spiritual love. There was a time in my youth when a misguided cleric loved me deeply and I pitied him. "I was so frivolous and blind that it seemed to me a virtue to be grateful and loyal to anyone who loved me. Damned be such loyalty that goes against the law of God! This is the kind of nonsense that goes on in the world, which makes no sense to me: that we consider it a virtue not to break with a friendship, even if the latter goes against God, whereas we are indebted to God for all the good that is done to us."[8]

Maria: You were able to enjoy close friendships with several spiritual directors, La Madre. Did some of them misunderstand your affectionate nature?

Teresa: "They, as God-fearing servants of the Lord, were afraid lest in any way I would become attached and bound to this love, even though in a holy way, and they showed me their displeasure. I laughed to myself to see how mistaken they were, although I didn't always express so clearly how little attached I was to anyone."[9] "After I beheld the extraordinary beauty of the Lord, I didn't see anyone who in comparison with Him seemed to attract me or occupy my thoughts."[10]

Maria: Yet you must admit, La Madre, that both Fray John of the Cross, whom you called "the Father of my soul," and Fray Jeronimo Gracian occupied your thoughts somewhat more than you would have liked at times.

Teresa: That is true. I loved them both deeply. Indeed, I teased Gracian about whether he loved me more than his mother! And I wrote to him, "Oh, Jesus, how wonderful it is when two souls understand each other!" But I was not blind to his faults. I corrected him for being "now...up in the air, now in the depths of the sea" and for not being careful to "tell the whole truth." Once in my amusement at his temperament I exclaimed, "Oh, my Father, it was quite unnecessary for you to swear, even like a saint, much less like a carter!"[11]

Maria: Gracian was a great help to you in your travels for the foundations. But he at times failed you, did he not?

Teresa: When he failed without notice or explanation to accompany me to Soria, I wrote that he had "made me sadder than I could have wished to be: it has been a great blow to me.... Everything will be distasteful to me now, for, after all, the soul feels the absence of one who both governs it and brings it relief. May all this conduce to God's service...!"[12]

Maria: Yet you understood only too well how integral a part of love was suffering disappointments, misunderstandings, and the failures of frail human beings—even those who had given their lives to God.

Teresa: As I wrote in my last letter to Gracian, "How little trust one can place in anyone but God." And, as my experience taught me, "All our troubles come from not keeping our eyes on Christ."

Maria: Your mention of troubles reminds me of how your love for your extended family also cost you a great deal, Mother. In the absence of your parents, your brothers and sisters relied on you to mother them and to assist in so many business matters they were unable to manage on their own.

Teresa: Oh, how they drained my time and energy! I wrote during my last years, "All the cares of my foundations put together have not made me as tired and depressed as these business matters.... I have been getting so worn out by my relatives."[13] But I love them so much. How could I refuse to help them? Poor Lorenzo had so much to endure. One of his sons had an illegitimate daughter and abandoned her. The other son married unwisely and went into perpetual debt. Then our brother Pedro, who suffered acute melancholia, went to live with Lorenzo and caused more tribulation.

Maria: Yet you did advise us, La Madre, not to become too involved with our relatives or to love them more than others.

Teresa: Indeed, daughter. "My own relatives were very fond of me...and I was so fond of them that I would not let them forget me. But I have learned...that it is God's servants who have helped me in trouble; my relatives, apart from my parents, have helped me very little.... Believe me...if you serve God as you should, you will find no better relatives than those [of His servants] whom His

Majesty sends you."[14]

Maria: I know you received many consolations from the love you experienced among your daughters of Carmel.

Teresa: You yourself were the foremost source of those consolations, dear Maria. I knew your faults. "Bad though you are," I wrote, "I wish I had a few more like you." How I wanted you to be my successor. My cousin Maria Bautista, in many ways your opposite, was a trial and a comfort. Her lively and intelligent correspondence moved me to say, "Almost everyone's letters tire me but yours." I was always grieved when I could not enjoy a chat with her. On the other hand, I had to correct her for being persnickety, willful and controlling. "If you would occasionally believe what I tell you," I said, "we should not get into so much trouble.... I don't know why you are so foolish."[15]

Maria: Our retreatants may be wondering if they would have had the stamina to survive your love, Mother.

Teresa: Well they might! "When I really love anyone, I am so anxious she [or he] should not go astray that I become unbearable."[16]

Maria: Never unbearable, Mother. But often irksome until we realized how determined you were that we grow in self-knowledge and love of God. I am sure we could all make Gracian's words our own: "But this love of mine for Mother Teresa, and hers for me, engendered in me purity, spirituality, and love of God, and brought her consolation and relief in her trials...."[17]

Teresa: Yes, such friendships are mutually profitable. But

"I have never...been able to tie myself to any friendship or to find consolation in or bear particular love for any other person than those I understand love Him and strive to serve Him; nor is it in my power to do so, nor does it matter whether they are friends or relatives. If I'm not aware that the person seeks to love and serve God or to speak about prayer, it is a painful cross for me to deal with him [or her]."[18]

Maria: How well that describes you, La Madre! Your ideal was "All must be friends, all must be loved, all be held dear." But to have to love those who showed no inclination to love God was ever a trial to you. Thank God your vocation surrounded you with friends of Christ.

Teresa: Thank God! Because "How great the consolation to find you are not alone. The two become a powerful help to each other in suffering and meriting. What excellent backing they give to one another."[19]

Teresa expressed her love for others through intercessory prayer, faithful correspondence with those from whom she was separated, and acts of service as varied as making woolen habits for her sisters and cheering the depressed by her animated presence. She was loved lavishly in return, especially by her Carmelite sisters who responded to her many departures with "great sadness and tears." Teresa admits "even though I forced myself as much as I could so as not to show it and I reprimanded them" for their grief at her parting, "this was of little help since their love for me is great, and in many ways it is obvious that this love is true."[20]

Because her own love was true, Teresa of Avila was able to help others by challenging them to reach for higher spiritual goals.

For Reflection

- *Are you a person who would find it extremely difficult to put into practice Teresa's directive:*

  "All must be friends, all must be loved, all be held dear"?

- *Consider: Whom do I have a great deal of trouble loving or deeply caring about? What may be the reasons for this difficulty? How might our retreat director's example be of some help? What response will I make to Teresa's witness?*

- *With friends who share your love for and commitment to Christ, how do you engender spiritual progress in one another? What more could you do to encourage each other to "love Him and strive to serve Him"?*

- *Listen to the word of the Lord and make of it what you will.*

  I give you a new commandment, that you love one another. Just as I have loved you, you also should love one another. By this everyone will know that you are my disciples, if you have love for one another.[21]

Closing Prayer

Lord,
let my love for you
be magnified by friends
whose hearts are lost
to you.
Amen.

Notes

1 *Living the Beatitudes: Daily Reflections for Lent from the L'Arche Daybreak Community*, (Cincinnati: St. Anthony Messenger Press, 1995), p. 13.

2 *Collected Works*, Vol. 3, *Poetry*, p. 380.

3 Ernest Kurtz and Katherine Ketcham, *The Spirituality of Imperfection: Storytelling and the Journey to Wholeness* (New York: Bantam, 1994), p. 30.

4 *Collected Works*, Vol. 1, *Life*, p. 194.

5 Ibid., Vol. 2, *Interior Castle*, 4.1.7.

6 Hughes, *Prison of Love*, p. 24

7 Peers, *Saint Teresa of Jesus*, p. 43.

8 *Collected Works*, Vol. 1, *Life*, p. 72.

9 Ibid., 325.

10 Ibid., p. 324.

11 Peers, *Saint Teresa of Jesus*, p. 76.

12 Ibid., p. 67.

13 Ibid., p. 56.

14 *The Way of Perfection*, p. 86.

15 Bielecki, *Mystical Writings*, p. 54.

16 Ibid.

17 Ibid., p. 72.

18 *Letters*, 24.6.

19 Ibid., 34.16.

20 Ibid., Vol. 3, *Foundations*, p. 248.

21 John 13:34-35.

DAY SIX

Giving Our Lives
Mission

Coming Together in the Spirit

A missioner needs a sense of humor. Witness the story told by Daniel Jensen, a Maryknoll priest serving in Guatemala. He was called on by a catechist to hear the first confessions of a group of second graders. Rather than occupying a confessional, Father Jensen sat down under a tree and invited the first penitent to join him. She did so, but said nothing.

"Do you want to go to confession?" he inquired kindly.

"Yes," she responded, saying nothing more.

Feeling a need to be a bit more directive, the priest said firmly, "Tell me your sins."

Without missing a beat, the seven-year-old replied, "The ones I did or the ones I plan on doing?"[1]

Defining Our Thematic Context

In her dialogue with Maria de San Jose, Teresa of Avila revealed the ways in which she gave her heart first to Jesus and then to others with whom she shared her love for him. Through affection openly expressed, direction freely given, and service selflessly provided, she warmed them at her inner fire. (Says Tolstoy, "The business of a Christian is everywhere and always one: To increase one's fire and let it give light to everyone.")

Teresa now turns her attention to that sustained love in evangelistic action we call mission. We will see how her holy wit sustained her on the road during her years as a pioneering foundress. And, in the process, we may be infected by her zeal for doing the impossible.

Opening Prayer

> Yours, you made me,
> Yours, you saved me,
> Yours, you endured me,
> Yours, you called me,
> Yours, you awaited me,
> Yours, I did not stray.
> *What do you want of me?*[2]

RETREAT SESSION SIX

Like the Maryknoll confessor in Guatemala, missioners of every ilk must expect the unexpected and be as flexible as a two-year-old on the jungle gym. Again drawing on Anthony de Mello's storehouse of instructive stories, we consider a case in point:

> A ship carrying a bishop on his way to a mission center stopped at a remote island for a day's rest. The bishop walked along the shore and came upon three fishermen mending their nets. He greeted them and they explained in Pidgin English that their people had been Christianized by missionaries

many years ago. Pointing to one another and beaming proudly, they said, "We Christians!" The bishop then invited them to say the Our Father. But they had never heard of it.

"What do you say, then, when you pray?" the bishop inquired.

"We lift eyes to heaven. We pray, 'We are three, you are three, have mercy on us,'" they responded.

Determined to leave these poor natives better off than he had found them, the bishop spent the day teaching them the Lord's Prayer. Before he departed, they gamely recited the entire formula without a single mistake.

Months went by before the bishop's ship once again approached that remote island. As he recited his evening prayers, the bishop fondly recalled the three fishermen and how he had patiently taught them. Suddenly he noticed a light moving toward the ship. As it came closer, he discerned three figures walking across the water. The fishermen called out to the bishop who, in awe and trembling, asked, "What is it you want?"

"Bishop," they said, "we so, so sorry. We forget lovely prayer. We say 'Our Father in heaven, holy be your name, your kingdom come...' then we forget. Please tell us prayer again."

Humbled, the bishop responded, "Go back to your homes, my friends, and each time you pray say, 'We are three, you are three, have mercy on us!'"[3]

Teresa of Avila, who taught that "all contemplation and perfection" are enshrined in the Our Father, would readily have recognized the fishermen without the words as true contemplatives. Her years on the road required her to communicate with mule drivers, inn keepers, wealthy property owners, crafty lawyers, municipal authorities, competitive buyers and competing religious founders from other orders. This "little old woman," as she termed herself, had to stretch far beyond the settled cloister life with those of her own kind.

In her mission as a foundress, Teresa manifested all the gifts Christ had been nurturing in her. She had a previously unknown capacity for sustained work despite her poor health. Her persuasive powers and administrative abilities ripened to the point where few could successfully oppose her for long. In the final fifteen years of her life, Teresa was so empowered and inspirited that it is exhilarating to retrace her steps in *The Book of Her Foundations*.

Her prologue assures us that the book contains no exaggerations or untruths of any kind; she is writing "for the praise of our Lord" and it is to him that all credit should be given. She apologizes for the "heaviness" of her style, saying, "I fear that I will become tiresome and tire even myself."

In a series of vignettes and observations, our retreat director reflects the holy wit of a woman with a mission who, despite all the unexpected turns in the road, made the primitive Carmelite Rule a reality in sixteenth-century Spain. Without financial backing or official approval, Teresa accepted the call.

Doing the Impossible

"I have often mentioned this, and now I repeat and ask that you always have courageous thoughts. As a result of them the Lord will give you grace for courageous deeds. Believe that these brave thoughts are important."[4]

The opposition to the founding of St. Joseph's in Avila was immediate and extreme. Some Carmelites agitated to have Teresa imprisoned for disobedience. The local citizenry tried to suppress the convent. A lawsuit was brought against Teresa, but she followed her courageous thoughts. St. Joseph's became the first of fourteen monasteries she would found before her final illness.

Not Without Complaint

> How is it, my God, that it's not enough that You keep me in this miserable life and that for love of You I undergo it and desire to live where everything hinders the enjoyment of You, in that I have to eat and sleep and carry on business and talk with everyone. How is it that when there is so little time left over to enjoy Your presence You hide from me? How is this compatible with Your mercy?[5]

She suffered it all, from fleas to floods and doubts that plagued her like hungry horseflies. So, like the psalmists before her, Teresa complained mightily to the Lord. However, her tone was often jocular, more like one lover teasing another to elicit an apologetic embrace than a disgruntled witness giving evidence of injustice. She says that love makes her "foolish" and she wonders how "the Lord puts up with it all."

Not Without Adversity

> Even though we did not travel during siesta time, I tell you, Sisters, that since the sun was beating on the wagons, getting into them was like stepping into purgatory. Sometimes by thinking of hell, at other times by thinking that something was being done and suffered by God, those Sisters journeyed with much happiness and joy.[6]
>
> I don't want to fail to mention the bad inn at which we stayed when I was in this condition [high fever]. We were given a small room with just a bare

tile roof. It had no window, and when the door was opened, the sun poured in everywhere.... The bed on which they made me lie down was such that I would have fared better on the ground. One part was so high and the other so low that one didn't know how to stay in it; it was like lying on sharp stones.[7]

When we hired guides, they led us along the good roads and then, saying they had other things to do, abandoned us shortly before we came upon the bad roads.[8]

After Teresa broke her arm and the prioress at Medina sent for a healer, the foundress quipped to a friend, "It cost her a great deal—and the treatment cost me a great deal too!"[9]

While they were crossing the Guadalquivir on a barge, the ropes broke loose and the barge went adrift. "I felt much more concern in seeing the anxiety of the boatman than I did about the danger. We were all praying; the others were all screaming."[10]

Hampered by Theologians

Arriving at Cordoba where they hoped to hear Mass without being seen by anyone, the sisters found themselves at an overcrowded church on Pentecost. They preferred to go away quietly rather than cause a stir by their unexpected and somewhat curious appearance. But Fray Julian de Avila insisted they remain.

And since he was a theologian we all had to follow his opinion.... We got out near the church, and although no one was able to see our faces, since we always wore large white veils in front of them, it was enough for the people to see us with veils, the white coarse woolen mantles we wore, and our sandals of hemp for them to get stirred up; and

that's what happened.... From the uproar of the
people you would think that a herd of bulls had
come into the church.[11]

When Teresa wanted to found a monastery without any
regular income, she received contradictory reactions. A
Dominican friar who had at first agreed now sent her
"two sheets of refutation and theology, in which he told
me that he had considered the matter carefully and urged
me against it. I replied that I had no wish to resort to
theology and could feel no gratitude for his learning in
this matter if it meant that I was not to follow my
vocation.... Some people began by telling me that they
approved of my plan, but afterward when they looked
into it further, they strongly urged me once more to give
it up. I told them that, in view of the speed with which
they changed their opinions, I preferred to stick to mine."[12]

Fending Off Critics

After one critic on the sidelines complained that the
foundress was not very brave, she told a friend, "He tells
me that I am like a mouse afraid of the cats."

The Andalusian Calced Carmelites, jealous of her
accomplishments with the Reform, spread rumors that
Teresa was going off to America. "I thought that was a
beautiful idea about sending me to the Indies.... God
forgive them: the best thing they can do is to say so many
things at once that nothing they say will be believed by
anyone."[13]

After Superior General Rubeo had caused her and her
friends so much trouble, Teresa writes him a letter that,
while disguised in sheep's clothing, has a wolf's bite: "If
only God would grant me the favour of hearing that your
Reverence was coming [here]! At the same time I should
be very sorry that you had to make such a trying journey.

So I shall have to wait for this happiness until that endless eternity, in which your Reverence will discover how much you owe to me."[14]

When the confessor at the Malagon convent, Don Gaspar de Villanueva, continues to oppose the acting-prioress, Teresa sends him packing with a velvet-covered gavel. "I shall be very sorry if you have to leave, but I realize that inward tranquillity is more important to you than pleasing me. May the Lord give us tranquillity, as He can. Amen."[15]

Our mentor's humanity is touching as she speaks of how she tries to be oblivious to the slings and arrows of critics. "Sometimes I think I am very detached; and as a matter of fact when put to the test, I am. At another time I will find myself so attached, and perhaps to some things that the day before I would have made fun of, that I almost don't know myself.... In like manner it seems to me that I don't care at all about things or gossip said of me; and when I'm put to the test this is at times true—indeed I am pleased about what they say. Then there come days in which one word alone distresses me, and I would want to leave the world because it seems everything is a bother to me."[16]

Teresa urges us not to dally or rationalize once Christ's call to a particular mission becomes clear. Despite "fleas, hobgoblins, and bad roads," despite language, cultural or other barriers, we have everything to gain by keeping on in the Lord's service. Jesus instructed Teresa: "Do what lies in your power; surrender yourself to me, and do not be disturbed about anything."

The more we act on our courageous thoughts, the more Christ will enable us to do. Rather than indulging our doubts, we should look past them to our ultimate destination. Teresa observes, "But during the little while this life lasts—and perhaps it will last a shorter time than each one thinks—let us offer the Lord interiorly and exteriorly the sacrifice we can."[17]

Armed with holy wit, trusting prayer and in the company of inspired companions, we can say "yes" to the mission whether it be forming a new kind of Christian community, educating for nonviolence, opposing the production of nuclear weapons or environmental pollution, creating havens for refugees or victims of abuse, working for economic justice, providing support for beleaguered families, or advocating long-term change in the Church. Without those three necessities, the Great Teresa herself would have been defeated.

For Reflection

- *Are you a person who generally greets the Lord's call to a particular mission with courage or temerity? Joy or dread? Doubts or trust? Self-confidence or convictions of ineptitude? Listen to Christ's words to Teresa:*

  "Do what lies in your power; surrender yourself to me, and do not be disturbed about anything."

- *Begin today to consider either how faithfully you are pursuing a present mission, or what new call may be awaiting. Decide how you will make your own the advice given to Teresa.*

- *What sources will you draw on (prayer, sacraments, music, poetry, videos, stories, companions) in order to "always have courageous thoughts" so that Christ will "give you grace for courageous deeds"?*

- *Listen to the word of the Lord and make of it what you will.*

  And he said to them, "Go into all the world and proclaim the good news to the whole creation."[18]

Closing Prayer

Lord,
send us out
with hearts of warriors,
winged hopes,
holy wit.
Amen.
What do you want of me?

Notes

1 "Mission Tales," Daniel Jensen, M.M. *Maryknoll Magazine*, July-August 1997, Vol. 91, No. 7.

2 *Collected Works*, Vol. 3, *Poetry*, p. 377.

3 Anthony de Mello, S.J., *The Song of the Bird* (New York: Doubleday, 1982), pp. 72-73.

4 Bielecki, *Mystical Writings*, pp. 87-88.

5 *Letters*, 37.8-9.

6 *Collected Works*, Vol. 3, *Foundations*, p. 224.

7 Ibid., pp. 224-25.

8 Ibid., p. 285.

9 Peers, *Saint Teresa of Jesus*, p. 76.

10 *Collected Works*, Vol. 3, *Foundations*, p. 225.

11 Ibid., pp. 226-27.

12 Green, p. 23.

13 Peers, *Saint Teresa of Jesus*, p. 76.

14 Ibid., pp. 69-70.

15 Ibid., p. 71.

16 *The Way of Perfection*, p. 252.

17 *Collected Works*, Vol. 2, *Interior Castle*, 7.4.14-15.

18 Mark 16:15.

DAY SEVEN

Living Lightly
'God Alone Suffices'

Coming Together in the Spirit

His monthly payments were long overdue. So Jones
wasn't surprised to receive a terse communication from
the furniture company. However, he was a bit put out by
the approach taken in the letter.

It read, "Dear Mr. Jones, What do you suppose your
neighbors would think if they saw one of our trucks
backing up to your front door to repossess all the
furniture you have neglected to pay for?"

A few days later the furniture company received the
following response from Jones. "Dear Sir, I have
discussed your question with all my neighbors to
ascertain what they would think. It is their unanimous
opinion that it would be a dirty trick by a heartless,
greedy company. Sincerely yours, Bill Jones."[1]

Defining Our Thematic Context

Holding things lightly was a skill Teresa of Avila
honed over a lifetime. Whether the "things" were
material possessions, the good opinions of others, the
certainty of doing things right, or the security of a
worldly estate, she was gradually liberated from all

entrapments. Thus, she was able to pursue Christ's mission with courageous thoughts and bare feet.

In our final session, Teresa invites us to do likewise— not because it is her way but Christ's way. We cling to so many things. Yet only one thing is necessary. As our mentor says, "Who possesses God/Nothing wants." Therefore, everything we need is already given.

Opening Prayer

> Let nothing trouble you,
> Let nothing affright you,
> All is fleeting,
> God alone is unchanging.
> Patience
> Everything obtains.
> Who possesses God
> Nothing wants.
> God alone suffices.[2]

RETREAT SESSION SEVEN

Like Teresa of Jesus, the saints who were gifted with holy wit engage us by their grasp of paradox. Having heard Augustine's maxim "who is not satisfied with God alone is much too greedy," we are not apt to forget it. The thirteenth-century mystic Meister Eckhart also had a memorable way with words. Said he: "A good man never complains of his misfortunes or distresses; he may only complain of his complaining—that he should be aware of it at all." Or the fourteenth-century mystic Julian of Norwich who observed, "Peace and love are always alive in us, but we are not always alive to peace and love."

Yet the voice that sings in closest harmony with Teresa's belongs to Saint Thomas More who lost his head rather than sell out his conscience to a king. His well-trained tongue did not desert him when Henry VIII had More imprisoned in the dreary Tower of London. On a visit to the Tower, Dame Alice, a practical-minded wife if there ever was one, tried to tempt Sir Thomas to submit to the king. The bait? His comfortable house with its well-stocked library and handsome grounds. But More would not be suborned by an earthly estate.

> I see no great cause why I should much joy either of my gay house or of anything belonging there unto, when, if I should but seven years lie buried under the ground and then arise and come thither again, I should not fail to find some therein that would bid me get out of doors and tell me it were none of mine. What cause have I then to like such a house as would soon forget his master?[3]

Teresa would have applauded More's elegant wit and firm resolve to live lightly—even as the executioner's axe lay ready.

As her parting gift to us, our retreat director presents a string of verbal diamonds that remind us "All that glitters is not worth grasping." She would convince us that "God alone suffices." (Her words elicit imagined responses from retreatants like ourselves.)

Letting Go of Honor

- "For these calumnies [by Carmelites who defamed her] not only failed to make me sad but gave me so great an accidental joy that I could not restrain myself."[4]

How did you just let go of your right to retaliate,

*Teresa? I get so incensed when people falsely accuse
me. And I feel justified in telling them off in no
uncertain terms. But maybe I'm missing something—
like the joy Jesus knew when he refused to retaliate
against his detractors. What a sense of freedom that
must give you! Not to be controlled by what others do
against you. I'll try to hold my "honor" a little more
lightly.*

Letting Go of Trifles

- "My God is not at all touchy. He doesn't bother
  about trifling things."[5]

*You know only too well, Teresa, how in the hothouse of
family life, "trifling things" shove us over the brink
into frustration with others. How many times have I
argued with my husband (or wife) about whether the
windows should be open or closed at night, yelled my
head off at the kids when they were "out of control,"
snapped at a sister or brother for a major offense like
not washing the car? The people we live with certainly
"chisel at us," as John of the Cross put it. Maybe it's
their vocation to remind us that our God "is not at all
touchy."*

Letting Go of Attachments

- "Oh, God help me, the silly things that come from
  such attachments are too numerous to be counted."[6]

*Like you, Teresa, I have been disillusioned many times
by my attachments to priests, religious and other
spiritual friends of whom I expected a great deal.
When some of them did not live up to my image of
them, I retreated into cynicism about human nature.
What I couldn't see was the injustice of my unrealistic
expectations, and the possessiveness they implied. I*

have clung to certain spiritual friends and been
devastated when they either had to leave or chose to
move on without me. How easy it is to forget that each
of us belongs to God alone.

Letting Go of Being Liked

- "Up until now, I thought I needed others, and I had
  more trust in help from the world. Now, I
  understand clearly that all this help is like little
  sticks of dry rosemary and that in being attached to
  it there is no security; for when some weight of
  contradiction or criticism comes along, these little
  sticks break.... I used to be very fond of being liked.
  No longer does being liked matter to me; rather, it
  seems in part to weary me, except in the case of
  those with whom I discuss my soul or whom I am
  thinking of helping. For I desire that the former like
  me so that they might bear with me and that the
  latter do so that they might be more inclined to
  believe what I tell them about the vanity of
  everything."[7]

What a hard teaching, Teresa! Surely you did not reach
this stage of enlightenment until late in life. I need the
approval of others so much that I even try to make
surly clerks in department stores and rude garage
mechanics like me. Some of my worst decisions have
resulted from the fact that I couldn't stand to do
something that would turn others against me. Maybe
your image of those little sticks of rosemary will help
me to take a few steps in the right direction.

Letting Go of Material Things

- "And I felt freedom in having so little esteem for
  temporal goods, for lack of these goods brings an
  increase of interior good. Certainly, such a lack

carries in its wake another kind of fullness and
tranquility."[8]

*Oh, Teresa, I envy your freedom. I have unwittingly
become addicted to buying things. Shopping somehow
makes me feel better about myself. I buy expensive
gifts for my children and grandchildren to prove that I
love them. And who can blame them if they have come
to expect it and hardly thank me anymore?*

*I've been robbing them—and myself—of the
recognition that our true worth has nothing to do with
possessions. Help me stand firm against the lure of the
mall, the shopping cart and the clever commercials.*

Letting Go of Security

- "Believe me...the means by which you think you are
  accumulating are those by which you will be
  losing."[9]

*When your Carmelite daughters wanted to require
large dowries of wealthy postulants, La Madre, you
called them back to poverty and trust. We may not be
vowed to poverty. But we live in a world where hunger
and homelessness exist to an unconscionable extent.
Yet we somehow think it is acceptable for the rest of us
to have more than we need—plus a bank account and a
retirement fund. Against Jesus' advice, we worry about
tomorrow—instead of sharing what we have today.
Help me to remember that the rich farmer who built a
bigger barn for his excess grain wound up dead in the
night with God's denunciation ringing in his ears.
(See Luke 12:16-21.)*

Letting Go of Property

- "Rather, it gives us great pleasure to find we are in a

house that we can be thrown out of, for we remember how the Lord of the world didn't have any."[10]

Come on, Teresa. Be reasonable. You know we can't let go of our houses. I'd be wrecked if I lost mine for any reason. Yes, I know it happens every day to the poor who are evicted, or the unemployed who go bankrupt or the family whose place is burned to the ground. But how do they stand it? I know the "Son of Man had nowhere to lay his head." However, he didn't have a family to worry about, did he? Maybe I'd better pray to Saint Thomas More for the holy wit to see that my house "would soon forget his master"!

Letting Go of Money

■ "What is there that can be bought with this money which people desire? Is there anything valuable? Is there anything lasting? If not, why desire it?... Oh, if all would agree to consider it as useless dross, how well the world would get on, and how little trafficking there would be! How friendly we should all be with one another if nobody were interested in money and honour! I really believe this would be a remedy for everything."[11]

Bull's-eye, Teresa! You've got this world's number. Money may not be the root of all evil—but it comes pretty close. Crime, greed, drug trafficking, political corruption, wars, social inequities, family squabbles— so much of our daily diet of bad news is generated by a lust for money. We forget that money has no more meaning than we agree to invest in it. As some humorist said, the trouble isn't that you can't take it with you, but that you can't even keep it while you're here. Pray for us, La Madre. We need to know that

*"where your treasure is, there your heart will be
also."*[12]

Our mentor concludes the dialogue with a smiled
blessing and a summary maxim: "All our troubles come
from not keeping our eyes on Christ."[13]

For Reflection

- *Are you a person whose self-worth, security or peace of
  mind is dependent on having "a little more" money,
  property or possessions than you actually need? Listen to
  Teresa:*

  "It is not money that will sustain us, but faith,
  perfection, and trust in God alone."[14]

- *Decide on one practical way you will begin to transfer your
  security from temporal goods to God alone.*

- *Reread Teresa of Avila's opening prayer for this day. Copy
  it in a journal, print it on a card, or create a poster
  illustrating it. Learn it by heart so that Teresa's wisdom is
  readily available to you when you need it.*

- *Listen to the word of the Lord and make of it what you
  will.*

  Come, buy wine and milk
    without money and without price.
  Why do you spend your money
      for that which is not bread,
    and your labor for that which does not satisfy?[15]

Closing Prayer

Lord,
you alone
do I need.
All else
is dross.
Untangle me!
Amen.

Notes

[1] Anthony de Mello, S.J., *The Heart of the Enlightened* (New York: Doubleday, 1989), p. 183.

[2] *Saint Teresa's Bookmark*, from *Collected Works*, Vol. 3, *Poetry*, p. 386.

[3] Richard Marius, *Thomas More: A Biography* (New York: Alfred Knopf, 1985), p. 234.

[4] *Collected Works*, Vol. 3, *Foundations*, p. 249.

[5] Bielecki, *Mystical Writings*, p. 151.

[6] *Collected Works, Way*, 4-8.

[7] Ibid., Vol. 1, *Spiritual Testimonies*, pp. 382-83.

[8] Ibid., Vol. 3, *Foundations*, p. 174.

[9] Ibid., p. 246.

[10] Ibid., p. 196.

[11] *Autobiography*, p. 201.

[12] Matthew 6:21.

[13] Bielecki, *Holy Daring*, p. 90

[14] Ibid., p. 107.

[15] Isaiah 55:1b-2.

Going Forth to Live the Theme

A Sufi mystic named Rumi once observed, "A saint is a theater where the qualities of God can be şeen." Teresa of Avila, having treated us to a profitable evening at the theater, reminds us that we, too, are called to progress along the royal road to holiness. Any Christian who excuses bad behavior by saying, "Well, I'm no saint," makes himself or herself a target for Teresa's arrows. "We may not be," she pointedly responds, "but what a good thing it is for us to reflect that we can be if we will only try and if God gives us His hand!"[1]

Prior to this retreat, our familiarity with Teresa's holy wit may have been confined to the possibly apocryphal story of the time her wagons were again stuck in the Castilian mud. She heard the divine voice saying, "Do you not know this is how I treat my friends?" To which Teresa retorted, "Well, no wonder you have so few!"

Now, having heard how forthrightly she expressed herself to God and others, we will recognize her voice in countless quips, maxims and candid prayers. There is something about an aged foundress who picks up a hammer and goes to work with the carpenters; then, when things go wrong, feels free to complain to the Lord "that either He not order me to get involved in repair works or He help me in this need."[2]

Teresa would have loved Dietrich Bonhoeffer's advice, written from a Nazi prison cell, "Spread *hilaritos* around you, and keep it yourself too!" Our retreat director knew that there is more than enough suffering to go around in the world. We need all the *hilaritos* we can get to grease the wheels of social interchange and heal the deadly seriousness that infects our practice of religion.

As a tribute to Teresa's holy wit, I close with an excerpt from "A Fool's Prayer":

> Father and God of Fools,
> Lord of Clowns and Smiling Saints,...
> I am grateful that Your Son, Jesus,
> who was this world's master of wit,
> daily invites me to be a fool for Your sake,
> to embrace the madness
> of Your prophets, holy people and saints.[3]

The retreat is over. We begin again to live by God's holy wit.

Notes

[1] *The Way of Perfection*, p. 122.

[2] Bielecki, *Mystical Writings*, p. 91.

[3] Fr. Edward Hays, "A Fool's Prayer," in Cal Samra, *The Joyful Christ: The Healing Power of Humor* (San Francisco: Harper & Row, 1986), pp. 50-51.

Deepening Your Acquaintance

The following books, tapes and videos are intended to help retreatants sustain their relationship with Teresa of Avila. Additional resources are included for those who want to explore the theme of holy wit.

Books

Bielecki, Tessa. *Holy Daring: An Outrageous Gift to Modern Spirituality from Saint Teresa, the Grand Wild Woman of Avila.* Rockport, Mass.: Element, 1994.

Bielecki, Tessa. *Teresa of Avila: Mystical Writings.* New York: Crossroad Publishing Co., 1994.

Cormier, Henri. *The Humor of Jesus.* New York: Alba House, 1977.

Delaney, John, J., ed. *Saints for All Seasons.* Garden City, N.Y.: Doubleday, 1978.

De Mello, Anthony, S.J. *Taking Flight.* New York: Doubleday, 1988.

_____. *The Heart of the Enlightened.* New York: Doubleday, 1989.

Green, Deirdre. *Gold in the Crucible: Teresa of Avila and the Western Mystical Tradition.* Dorset, England: Element, 1989.

Hutchinson, Gloria. *Six Ways to Pray From Six Great Saints*. Cincinnati: St. Anthony Messenger Press, 1982.

Samra, Cal. *The Joyful Christ: The Healing Power of Humor*. San Francisco: Harper & Row, 1986.

The Autobiography of St. Teresa of Avila, trans. E. Allison Peers. Garden City, N.Y.: Doubleday, 1960.

The Collected Works of St. Teresa of Avila, Vols. One, Two, Three, trans. Kieran Kavanaugh, O.C.D. and Otilio Rodriguez, O.C.D. Washington, D.C.: ICS Publications, 1976-1985.

The Way of Perfection, St. Teresa of Avila. trans. E. Allison Peers. Garden City, N.Y.: Doubleday, 1964.

Audio Resources

Guidance in Prayer from Three Women Mystics (Julian of Norwich, Teresa of Avila, Therese of Lisieux), by Margaret Dorgan, O.C.D. Kansas City, Mo.: Credence Cassettes.

Way of Perfection: Teresa of Avila, read by Juliana Clapp. Kansas City, Mo.: Credence Cassettes.

Videos

Teresa of Avila: Personality and Prayer, series by Fr. Thomas Dubay. Ft. Collins, Colo.: Ignatius Press.